INCREDIBLE LOVE POEMS
And OTHER PASSIONATE WRITINGS

INCREDIBLE LOVE POEMS
And OTHER PASSIONATE WRITINGS

Thomas Joe Franks, Ph.D.

Rev. date: 07/17/2019

To order additional copies of this book, contact:
Xlibris
1-888-795-4274
www.Xlibris.com
Orders@Xlibris.com
799348

Dedication

I dedicate this book to Karen Lovejoy and our family. We have truly been blessed with the grace and mercy of God the Father, God the Son, and God the Holy Spirit. Many of YOU have inspired me to go forth with an even greater determination, boldness and zeal. To you I say, "THANKS".

In my prayers, I thank God for you and our Christian heritage. I appreciate many of you sharing your thoughts with me. You are indeed on the cutting edge. YOU have tremendous POSSIBILITIES.

Many of the poems are about Karen, my lovely wife, companion, and best friend...Some of the poems may contain adult language. The majority of the poems were written before and after our marriage.

First Words

For several years. I have wanted to write a book of poetry. I think you will be intrigued by the simplicity of these poems. Part 1 deals with POEMS that I have written to Karen over the past 17 years and some other inspirational poems as well. Romantic relationships are the spice of life. They make us feel so alive. Genuine romance comes when two people show that they truly care for each other. Acts of kindness and unselfish affection make us feel loved and appreciated. Romance is the key to keeping the sparks alive and growing a relationship that will never lose its shine.

Part 2 deals with motivational poems and other PASSIONATE WRITINGS that I think you will enjoy. Some of the poems may be a little risqué, but nothing like the language on TV or the movies of today.

This is no ordinary book of poetry. It's about two people in love who later got married and continued to share their thoughts and emotions. I appreciate so many of you sharing your thoughts with me. The POSSIBILITIES are limitless. I thank God for my lovely wife, companion, and best friend...Karen.

Previously, I have written fictional books, inspirational books, religious books, and motivational books. This was a real challenge. But I love poetry and classical prose. Hopefully, you will find a favorite poem that you like. This book is filled with passion, energy, and vitality. Enjoy!

PART 1

My Heart as a Poet
By Thomas Joe Franks

We must walk freely my Love.
Any fences must be torn down,
Our feelings must be spoken to each other!
We must love as the warmth of the sun.
Our faith and love to each other are incredible!
Our huge beacon of love yearns for the other...
We know that heaven awaits us someday.
We take heed. We love. We embrace.
We are not blinded by our own deeds.
Our hearts are no longer alone in the park.
We have rescued each other from the dark!

No fear is in our hearts.
Our responsibility...our promises we keep.
We are through with heartache and blame.
We have truly learned how to love one another.
We believe in the other.
The path is bright ahead.
You, my Love, have brought life and breath into my soul.
I honor you! I love you! I cherish you.
Faith and Love have surrounded us.
We are free indeed.
Our hearts are soft, tender, and gentle as can be!

Our wells are full.
Our lights do shine.
The angels are looking on...
They sing.
The heart of this poet lives on...
Within the walls of your heart, I am alive.
You are a well-watered garden...

You have blossomed into a beautiful Princess.
Your bouquet of faith and honesty grows strong.
Your walls have come down like the ancient city of Jericho.
You (Karen) will always be welcomed in my heart
Forever and always!

To Karen My Love
By Thomas Joe Franks

When the sun comes up in the morning,
Guess who I want to have by my side?
Right on...You, my sweet Princess!
At the start of each day from henceforth,
I want you there with me...bringing me coffee, etc. (Ha!)
That would be the start of a perfect day!
To open my brown eyes each morning
And see you there beside me...will be so wonderful.
You have made my dreams come true,
And I have decided to let my heart rule.
One Day With You, My Lovely Karen
Is all it took for me to be hooked!
Just to start my day with you
Is absolutely incredible and FUN-tastic.
Looking at you wake up with those emerald green eyes,
And stretching your arms around me...
And holding me so tight...
Watching you squirm as I kiss you passionately,
One Day With You makes everything seem so right!
Knowing that when I go to work,
I have the thought of you waiting for me upon my return.
This makes my day! Waiting, yet anticipating your love...
And your sweet lips upon mine!
To rush home to you and open the door...
Seeing you there before me dressed so elegantly in time,
And motioning me to come over and make love to you...
This is all so breathtaking.
One Day plus 50 years...With You...is all I'm praying for!
When I look at you, I feel such a tingle inside,
Especially, when I see the sparkle
In your emerald green eyes!

Every part of my being reaches out to you...
To love you, caress you, hold you,
And observe your beauty.
This is why I need One Day With You...
Every day for the next 50 years!
It is not by coincidence, happenstance, or accident
That we lovingly and tenderly met.
Time, destiny, hope, and God brought us together.
Our time is getting better and richer
As we spend it with one another...And most of all,
It is bringing us closer and closer together forever!
PS: When you love me, be tender
And gentle with me because
I like it slow! Promise me! Loving you, Thomas Joe

My Special Angel
By Thomas Joe Franks

You are my secret angel.
You have kept me from a lot of trouble.
I feel your presence when you are near.
You are always such a dear.
Without you near, life would be so unclear.

You are my special angel...
I am so overwhelmed with your beauty.
You seem to always be on duty.
You seem to always know what to do.
With you so near, I am never blue.
Life is so sweet and true with you.

You are my loving angel.
You seem to know when danger is near.
But with you so near, I have nothing to fear.
My Darling angel, I love you, it is clear.
With you around, it will be a great year.

You Are My Everything
By Thomas Joe Franks

You remind me of the sun
That always shines so vibrantly throughout the day.
You give me stability that keeps me straight every day.
You are the full moon that gives me light during the night.
You are stars that always shine ever so brightly.
You are like the oxygen that I breathe. I am alive.

You always keep my heart beating
Sometimes slow… sometimes fast.
Your love to me is like an ocean…deep…yet refreshing.
Your love is like a red, red, rose
That has natural beauty that continues to grow.
My message to you is simple…I will always love you.

You remind me of a Blue Bird
That always has a song to sing.
If I could sing, I would sing "You are my everything".
I will always be glad that you are in my future.
I want you to always be with me for the rest of my life.

If You Could…
By Thomas Joe Franks

If you could see the inside of my soul
And the inside of my heart…
You would know that you and I are very special friends.
I will not pretend. You are a very special blend.

If you could see the inside of my head,
And see my passionate emotions like butter on bread…
And know my thoughts,
You would know how I cherish you
More than fine gold wrought.

If you could see all the ways you reassure me in life,
The way you talk, look, and listen without strife.
The way you know just what to say and do…
You encourage and dispel any kind of fear that may accrue!

The sparkle in your beautiful emerald green eyes…
Both your smiles, laugh, and your touch…
Are just a few of the many reasons that you mean so much!
Karen, I love you and your soft common touch.

Knowing we can talk to each other
About any and everything as such.
We know that together we will get through our life's journey
Because life has brought us so much.

If I could search the whole world over…
Know this one thing…
I could never find another friend so kind and true.
We have love beyond the morning dew.

Though with each new day and with each new sunrise,
We may not know what's in store for us...
But there is one thing we do know for sure,
Each day we know that we are special and will endure.

So if you could see the inside of my head and heart,
You would see my thoughts and compassion
Like butter on bread and a cherry tart.
I am so blessed to have you as my lover and best friend.
Love and Friendship are like the breeze
Of palm trees, gold, and diamonds to impart.

You are friendly, kind, caring, and understanding.
You are sensitive, loyal, humorous, fun, and secure.
You are always there...this is true!
Karen, I would like to be the sort of friend
That you have been to me. Amen!

To My Dearest Karen:
My Valentine Treasure
By Thomas Joe Franks

A Valentine Treasure is a Queen like you.
Who has so often crossed my mind
Until I lost all track of time.
Diamonds glisten in the sunshine,
However you sparkle not only in the springtime
But all year long, especially as my Valentine.

The warmth of your love is like a hundred sparks of light.
Your love for me is ever so bright.
No matter how long we are together,
You will always be my Valentine Treasure.
Each part of you is like a luminous
And dazzling precious stone
That gleams and glows like a queen on her throne!

Valentines come in all shapes and sizes,
Yet each one has a loving treasure
That brings so much pleasure.
I am so fortunate to have met you and married you.
Being with you, I will never be blue.
I am going to stick with you like a pound of glue.
And then I'll look at you and enjoy the view.

A Valentine Treasure is a Queen like you.
Who has so often crossed my mind
Until I lost all track of time.
Diamonds glisten in the sunshine,
However you sparkle not only in the sunshine and springtime
But all year long, especially as my Valentine.

I can't stop thinking about how sexy you are.
You looked so hot this morning. I was almost on fire.
As you were getting dressed, I must confess
That I was very impressed with your body…like Mae West.
Mmmm…Hmmm...
I can still taste your sweet lips with so much zest.

The Gift of Love To Karen
By Thomas Joe Franks

A gift can be for a Birthday…Anniversary…or Christmas.
A gift may be flowers, chocolates, or a diamond ring.
Gifts are normally from a passionate heart…
Sometimes from a heart that is crying out.
I was so blue before I met you.
I was touched by an angel…
The Lord gave me you.
You are the gift of passion and Herculean strength.
I admire you as a gift of faith.
My heart will always belong to you.

Gifts of happiness and joy cannot be destroyed.
Life sometimes is like a merry-go-round.
Yet, we can get off at any moment.
Love is the gift of family and memories shared…
Love is wisdom, understanding, and knowledge so rare.
My incredible gift to you, I cannot hide.
Sometimes, I feel like I am on a roller coaster ride.
My spontaneous gift to you comes from deep inside.
My love is deep…deeper than the ocean blue.
My gift is the incredible gift of love that I give to you.

The Green-eyed Lady (Karen)
St Patrick's Day
By Thomas Joe Franks

You are a beautiful green-eyed lady of kindness and love.
You have a big heart for others…
Whom you are always thinking of.
I love your smile which makes your eyes shine with twinkles.
Your giggles and laughs will always
Make you young without wrinkles.

I love the way you hug me and hold me close!
Sometimes, you will stare at my wooly face
And smile the most.
You mean more to me than anything in life!
I am so happy the Lord gave you to me as my loving wife.

Heretofore, I had looked for love in so many wrong places.
Now, I find love in your eyes when I look into your face.
I love to think about our wonderful times in Germany…
The land of paradise.
I will never take you for granted. You always look so nice.

Today, my heart sings love songs of joy
Because you are in my heart!
I miss you so much when we are apart.
You need to know that I am always here.
You will never need to lack for anything or be in any fear.

You gave me your heart and I to you!
I will always love you and stick with you like glue.
I think of you every day in my loving arms.
You are my St Patrick's Day green-eyed charm!

A Brand New Day Has Dawned!
By Thomas Joe Franks

To the two of us, the past may be just a dim distant star!
However, from henceforth, our universe
Will be full of life... and candy bars.
Shining ever so passionately and brightly.
Why? Because you and I are stars because of who we are!
Our memories together are so precious
To our tender hearts.
We have touched each other like no one
Has ever done before.

I love caressing your beautiful and elegant face and body,
Especially during the early morning hours...
Hearing the birds singing our songs.
The sun gently comes through our curtains,
And the morning air is so cool and refreshing
Until it takes our breath away.
We know that each day will be brighter
As we continue our love always.

We eventually awaken in each other's arms.
We talk. We whisper. We giggle. We laugh. We have fun!
We know that we have traversed
Many mountains in our lives.
Now, it is time to relax...
To enjoy the moments...
Especially, the incredible times
We had together born of the gentle breeze of warmth.
Today, we will play and dance and live.
And we will love passionately like a wind storm.

Loving You Passionately...

You Are the Reason
By Thomas Joe Franks

When I look into your emerald green eyes,
I see a thousand stars in the sky.
You are the reason my world continues to turn.
You are the smile on my face.
You are my dreams and my hope.
I love holding you in my arms.
I can't resist your charm.
When my day is not okay,
You come and make me happy as a day in May.
When I feel the world crashing down on me,
You're the one I need.
You are the reason...my world, my life, my everything.
My sweet green eyed lover,
I will always be yours.
You are the start of a perfect day.

Today is a good day!
By Thomas Joe Franks

Today is a good day!
How could anything go wrong?
It's a good day for rolling along.
It's a good day for singing a song.
It's a good day for getting things done!
It's a good day for having some fun!
It's a good day for helping someone!
It's a good day for dying my long curly hair.
It's a good, good, good, good day!
Have a GREAT FUN DAY!

Love is So Incredible!
By Thomas Joe Franks

Karen, sometimes, our love is just too incredible
For any simple, easy, or complicated definition or explanation.
Our love is rapidly growing…part me and part you.
Sometimes, love is explosive.
Love should always bring
Happiness, joy, delight, and stability.
Love can sometimes be very serious,
Comforting, beautiful, and incredible.
Love is bigger than the two of us.
Love is a many splendored and beautiful thing.
Love goes deeper than our senses. Colors are brighter.
Smells are more aromatic and fragrant.
Food taste even more delicious
When two people are "in love".
Our sense of touch should bring feelings of pleasure.
Hearing your sweet voice whispering in my ear saying,
"I love you"…
Will cure the pain in my tender heart.
Seeing your beautiful face again will take my breath away.

Our Love is So Incredible!
Even though our love is serious,
We will find time to be funny and humorous.
During this particular time in history,
Laughter is therapeutic, beneficial, and restorative.
My plan is to make you smile and laugh a lot.
What is love without laughter?
What is a day without sunshine?
What is love without humor?
Our love is Incredible because
We are the best of friends as well.

At first, our love was like a secret thing,
But this was only temporary.
There came a time when I had to tell the world...
Show the world...
That you are mine and I am forever yours.
That day came and now our Love is so Incredible!
Even though time is standing still right now,
Our love is not like some clock.
We cannot take it apart and see what makes it tick.
It just is. Our love is.

Our Love is So Incredible! That's it.
We have no extemporaneous measuring devices
That are capable of measuring our love.
It's too Incredible.
But love has found us as two people
Worthy of love and being loved.
Sometimes, love doesn't make much sense.
On the other hand, it is the only thing that makes any sense!
Our Love is So Incredible!
How do I know that I love you with all of my heart?
It's simple, not complicated. I have loved you from the start...
The very first time I laid eyes on you.
Even though, I have written
Perhaps hundreds of poems in the past,
I now have a new kind of poetry in my heart for you!
I feel as if I could write ten thousand poems...
Just about you and me.
As I said, Our Love is So Incredible.

Love is So Incredible! (Part 2)
By Thomas Joe Franks

My poems have deeper meaning,
Beauty, loveliness, elegance,
And exquisiteness now…All because of you, My Love.
There are so many reasons that I love you.
That's why I married you.
Now I can tell you all the reasons "I love You"
For the next 50 years…or so.
Our Love is So Incredible.
OUR TIME IS NOW.
The past is gone.
The present and future are ours.
Our time is real. OUR TIME HAS COME.
Our rainbow of precious love is greater than any pot of gold.
Our dreams are being fulfilled before our very eyes.
Perhaps, I'm beside myself. Perhaps, I am unique.

Perhaps, I am a Romantic. Perhaps!
But I got to tell you, our time has come.
It doesn't really matter what we are doing
As long as we are doing it together…
Whether it's talking, walking,
Dreaming, traveling, holding hands,
Smiling, laughing, crying,
Or just enjoying each other's company.
Our Love is So Incredible!
Some people are cautious with their love.
They measure it out as if it is going to be all used up.
They think that when it is gone, there won't be anymore!
This is absurd and ridiculous. Why?
Because LOVE is not that way at all…

Just the opposite.
The more love we give away to one another,
The more love we have in return.
This "treasure" called love
Always replenishes itself… always.
How happy I am to know right now that we are "in love"
And our time has come!
I need you so desperately. Our Love is So Incredible!

Somebody Loves You Exceedingly!
By Thomas Joe Franks

Somebody Loves You Exceedingly, don't you see?
My thoughts are with you, I guarantee.
Somebody really and truly cares...
You are always in my prayers.
I truly love you, I do declare!
Our love for one another is free
Not only in Florida, but also in Tennessee.
Soon we will have a grand old jubilee
As we sit together and drink high tea.

Somebody Loves You Exceedingly,
And that would be me!
Ever since that night you kissed me,
I have had my eye on thee.
Never doubt for a moment that this is not true.
I'm in love with you like two Zebras in a zoo.
You are a rare treasure indeed,
You are a special woman of beauty and breed.
I love you, I must confess and concede.
Our wholesome love will certainly succeed!

Somebody Loves You Exceedingly.
I have faith in our love and truly believe...
That we will go forth and greatly achieve.
Today, we are young.
We will never get old, but may grow older.
And our love will never grow cold.
One day we will look back and laugh with content,
We will know that our lives together have been well spent.
Even during the changing scenes of life,
I will be your gentle husband...and you, my lovely wife.

Together, we will live an incredible fantasy life
Without a bunch of silly strife. I love you incredibly!

Somebody else loves you MORE than you will ever KNOW.
Somebody else is always thinking of you wherever you go.
Somebody else really and truly cares.
Somebody else loves you beyond compare.
And is concerned about every aspect of your welfare.
Never doubt for a moment
That you are in the Lord's prayers.

You are a rare TREASURE and a tremendous FIND.
Let us not waste any more time,
In getting to know the Lord during this lifetime.
So please believe me when I say,
"Somebody else loves you incredibly today."
And that somebody else is Jesus Christ ALWAYS!

A Star Is Born

By Thomas Joe Franks

The Good Lord took a star from the night
And in her eyes, He put much light.
She has great wisdom and understanding down here.
God's rainbow has touched her tears.
Karen has a special glow
That only God fully knows.
God conferred with Himself and thought for a while
And then decided to give her warm sunshine for her smile.
He planted a beautiful bouquet of love in her heart
Which we could smell the aroma as a work of art.
The storms, rains, and windy weather
Have come and gone…
Only to find her a most delicious plum in God's Kingdom.
God has blessed her with talents and abilities
That belong only to kings, queens, and royalty.
Thank You God. You have made my day.
My life is now easier along the way.

My Secret of Loving You (Part 1)
By Thomas Joe Franks

One day, long ago, I finally accepted
My limitations and shortcomings.
I found out that I was in fact a human being
Who made mistakes many times in many ways!
That's when I began to realize that the acceptance
Of another's love was what I so desperately needed to
Enrich and enhance my life in my own personal growth.
Yes, I began to see myself in love with
A very special woman without a lot of entangled distractions.
I began to let love grow inside my tender heart.
I also began to trust, have faith in, and love another person
And express my true feelings in a very real and genuine way.
Our authentic feelings, tangible needs, and heartfelt
Boundaries were discussed.

In loving you, I realized that I had chosen a classy lady
In whom I admire and highly respect.
I will protect you and shelter you from any outside harm.
My consciousness of you
And your beauty has risen to new heights.
My tender heart has opened so naturally
For you and your love!
I must tell you that I believe that my love
Is deeper and more passionate
Than any man that you have ever met.
In my heart, I do not think that you will ever find
A deeper and more mature love than mine.
My heart is now open to your eternal spring of love.
You have given new meaning to my enthusiastic life.
My Secret of Loving You is You...My Dear Sweet Wife!

You are different than any other woman on Planet Earth.
You are more SPECIAL
Than any other woman on Planet Earth.
God threw away the mold whenever He created you!
I am glad!
You do not march to another's drum.
You do things your way. I like this in you.
The flow of your love fills my receptive
And passionate heart.
As our hearts love one another,
We are still learning to appreciate the other.
We are still learning to communicate with the other.
We take nothing for granted or assumption.
Our Love resides because truth is expressed.
My Secret of Loving You is your Truth
And genuine Expression!
Darling, today accept my true love for you
As it is given and whenever it is given.

My Secret of Loving You (Part 2)
By Thomas Joe Franks

I truly know that you will always appreciate my love for you
Because it is my precious, unconditional gift to you!
I know that you will continue to acknowledge my love daily.
Why? Because we both will always keep
Our love alive for each other...
Loving passionately, loving fully, loving completely.
I promise to put no attachments ahead of you...
No needs ahead of you.
I want our love to continuously grow.
My Dearest Princess, you are like a well of overflowing love.
Love radiates through you.
As you stand in front of the mirror,
Love reflects through every fiber
Of your body, spirit, and soul.
My Secret of Loving You is You, My Dear Princess!

Yesterday With Karen!
By Thomas Joe Franks

It seems like only yesterday
When we met with great expectations
And magical moments.
We had thoughts and words of whispered promises...
Filled with special romantic moments.
Do not worry. Do not fret!
We are not in the desert.
The stars are too bright for that.
Our nights will soon be filled with magical autumn light!

When our eyes first met,
Your hair sparkled and glistened in the evening moonlight.
The secret is still hope and love...And "never giving up".
We will make it through this as well.
I remember yesterday
When we played in the snow in Europe.
It was so crisp, white, and a little chilly...
And I acted a little silly.

We were two children in our own playground,
Where I made angel wings in the snow.
You were so fresh...fresh as a daisy.
And you still are!
The fallen drifts of deep snow
Are still waiting for our return.
Wasn't that a magical snowy day when we threw
Snowballs at each other...Along the way?

We did not get wet and cold.
We were too hot for each other.
Oh, the joy of being together and in love. We still are!
Our nights were passion filled with delight.

We cuddled under the blanket as we watched...
The flames of the candles flickering in the night.
The mornings were cozy and brisk...
As the sunlight filled our bedroom.
Our deep and special love will last for all time...
Yesterday, today, and forever!

My Distant Love (Part 1)
By Thomas Joe Franks

The long nights are getting warmer.
It's a little chilly without you here
By my side as my transformer.
I know I will see you soon, oh yeah!
But I can't help wishing you were near me now.
Since knowing you, my Love, the stars shine so brightly.
Even the night sky seems to be speaking so politely.
I close my eyes...I see you.
You are special and precious in my thoughts, it's true!

Our distant love must get better.
Our moments together have been an open letter.
Sometimes I pretend
That your loving arms are wrapped around me
As my lover and best friend!
As you hold me tight, you feel so sexy.
I feel peaceful tonight as our two souls ignite!
It just feels right being with you tonight...
As your emerald green eyes sparkle like the dew.

Happiness, excitement, and warmth so divine,
Are locked up in your ruby red lips that taste like sweet wine.
As your kisses press against my lips so gently,
My heart melts so intently.
My toes tingle.
My whole world jingles.
I feel so ecstatic.
Recent changes and love filled moments
Have been so intense!

Your presence is reassuring...Your style has such class.
As I close my eyes, you are there at last.

As I open my eyes, you disappear.
My Distant Love, we must be together soon on my frontier.
Without you here, this little apartment
Is cold and empty as a spoon!
I sit here alone and discrete under the moon...
Knowing you will be back in my arms of heat.
And my life will again be complete!

Tonight, I will close my eyes.
I will hold you close to my thighs.
I will pretend it's a mid-summer night's dream!
Distance has stolen my dear Karen away, it seems.
I sit. I stand. I lie down.
My love for you expands.
I cannot sleep. What is wrong with me?
I'm in love with a "woman" from Tennessee!

My Distant Love (Part 2)
By Thomas Joe Franks

My thoughts of you are elaborate, it's true.
You are my Princess from 5th Avenue.
As you know, I am NOT a toy,
But I certainly like to bring you a lot of joy!
Wind me up so that I can love you all night long.
I yearn for your tender touch so strong.
I need your sweet kisses.
One day, you are going to be my lovely Mrs.

I miss our early mornings together
As I jump around like a jack rabbit in good weather.
I truly miss you.
You are my best friend, it's true.
I will be with you 'til the end.
As I talk to you on the telephone, I pretend
That you are by my side again!
Baby, I just want to be with you and blend.

You are my Darling.
You will always be my "woman".
You will always have such style and flare.
We will listen to our favorite songs without despair.
Soon, I will be free to be in your loving arms always.
We are two souls made for the intricacies of love.
Even though distance may separate us like two doves,
Our love will transcend the very stars above.

Nothing can really keep us apart,
Because we are meant to be together like a horse and cart.
The wind, rain, sleet, snow, and hail
May come and go, we know full well,

But I'll always love you as my Southern Belle.
You have become that beautiful woman I know.
You have touched my tender heart and soul.
As the soul mate who cares, you have made me feel whole!

I Am Incredibly Yours!
By Thomas Joe Franks

Karen, over the last few months
As we have exchanged so many words,
Ideas, concepts, and brilliant colors on a canvas of paint...
We have spoken comfortably at a distance...
Through computer modems, keyboards,
Cards, telephones, and letters.

First, we communicated small talk
And a few long distance "hello's"...
Many pleasantries, unexpected confessions...
And later, such admiration and desire
With so much passion.
Neither have we been silent in our secrets revealed.

We savor the sweetness of our words together
Because our Love has grown to something
Much finer, richer, and deeper.
Sometimes, an excited rush of words, poems,
Lyrics of songs, or experiences
Have come forth like an artesian well
Under a hot burning sun!

I'm looking forward to the brilliance of your beautiful smile,
Your playful green eyes, your beautiful soul, and sweet spirit.
I treasure your words through your sexy voice.
I have fallen like a star from the sky into your lovely arms.

I Am Incredibly Yours! As soon as we meet,
There will be many more exciting and incredible words...
Our enchanted eyes will meet again,
And our lips will whisper...
A language too ancient for computers and cell phones.

A Love Like Ours Is Hard To Beat
By Thomas Joe Franks

As we take note of who we are...And where we are today,
We notice that we are a long ways from where we began.
We have surpassed our dreams
In so many ways and phrases.
We both shine so brightly now
That you have become my cat's meow!
You are my brilliant star who is the hottest by far.

You warm me and inspire me...You are an inspiration to me.
So many times, you are the source of my dreams.
As we travel, I see your smile that beams.
A Love Like Ours Is Hard To Beat...
You have made my life complete!

The speed of time moves ever so quickly,
Days turn to weeks...Weeks to months...And months to years.
Our tears and fears have turned to joy and cheers.
No more sadness for us...
Thus, our lives together is one big PLUS.
Our courage is filled with laughter like kids on a school bus!

A Love Like Ours Is Hard To Beat...
Beyond our wildest dreams!
When I'm with you, I feel the sunshine...Even in the rain!
You feed my soul with kindness,
Where there has been so much pain.
With you, my world is full...
It makes me want to sing and shout with everything to gain.

Walk close beside me...Let me help guide you.
Lean on me... I will take your hand
And kiss it because you're a queen!

I do understand you. I do love you. We will never part.
You are always in my heart. I have loved you always,
Always... right from the start.

You are the one I want to be with...
You are the one who has my heart.
I really love your smile and laughter...
Your soul, your personality, and your body too.
I feel so whole when I'm with you.

When your lips touch mine...I feel so refined.
The smile on your face every morning is like a gold mine.
Thoughts of you go through my mind all the time.
A Love Like Ours Is Hard To Beat...
We are partners until the end...All my Love I do send!

Put Your Sweet Lips A Little Closer To Mine

By Thomas Joe Franks

When I think of your luscious body so close to mine,
It makes me more refreshed than sweet strawberry wine.
You are my sweet lady so refined,
Our passionate embrace is so divine.
You are heaven to me...and are always on my mind.
I remember your elegant kisses near the castle on the Rhine.

Your seductive touch gives me chills down my spine!
You are sweet, sexy, sensual, and delightful all the time.
As you put your sweet lips a little closer to mine,
It feels like hot liquid fire in my blood line.
I do believe that your beautiful human design
Came straight from the Heavenly Vine.

Yes, I get impatient sometimes...OK, a lot of times.
But you certainly know that I would walk the line...
Any time to experience such an
Intoxicating feeling of your love so fine.
Do I live in a fantasy world of thine?
Let's talk about satin sheets, rose petals,
And whip cream on cloud nine
As you put your sweet lips a little closer to mine.

Your seductive kisses and warm hugs combine
And seem to say to me, "Sweet Love, come and dine"!
Let us experience a perfumed candle light and more wine.
My heart beats ever so fast, but I do not whine.
My erogenous zones of passion are on the rise again...
As you put your sweet lips a little closer to mine!

Put your sweet lips close to mine.
Put your head on my shoulder…
That's where it belongs.
I will wrap myself around you…ahh so tight.
I will whisper in your loving ear…
I love you, Karen so dear.

Those words can't come close
To describing your tender touch.
I feel so good when you are near.
My love for you surges when you are by my side.
I know we have a love that will last…
Our love is a blast and will never end because our souls are
United and our lives are ignited. You are my love forever.

My Love for You
By Thomas Joe Franks

Actions speak louder than words,
But they cannot adequately describe the emotion and love
I feel in my heart for you.
No matter how hard I try to express my emotions to you,
They seem to fall short of my passionate expressions
That I have for you.
Love is the strongest emotion possible.
I wish that I could express all my feelings of love to you.
Love is an emotion unlike any other. It is so patient and kind.
I am learning to be more patient,
Yet I know I have a ways to go.

True love is an incredible feeling.
I am now experiencing that kind of feeling
And emotion with you.
I know I truly love a woman who shares
The same feelings I do.
I think you do understand how much I love you.
Love is one of the most difficult emotions to handle...
Yet for me, patience is too!
I know that with love come mistakes at times...
That sometimes you wish
You could take back. Besides finding God,
You are the greatest thing
That has happened to me in over 50 years.
I am so glad that we have so
Much in common, yet we are different.
This makes life even more exciting!

I Know You Are There!
By Thomas Joe Franks

I can smell the sweet fragrance in your hair,
Especially when I run my fingers through it as you are aware!
The warmth of your body feels like honey.
It makes my heart feel so sunny.
I can see the sparkle in your eyes.
They are emerald green so beautiful and so alive.
I wish I could honestly sing,
I would serenade you and give you another ring.

Your voice is soft when you speak to me,
I get so excited...It's like London "High" tea.
Harrod's is probably the place to be!
We have both come a long ways from Tennessee.
Sometimes, your kisses taste like London strawberry jam...
As I kiss you slowly and passionately...as a lion, not a lamb!
I know this is not a dream
Because we both generate too much steam.

The fire within us is more than a flame
As passion ignites our human frames.
In the night, I hear myself whisper your name.
Our lives are much more than any London game.
My desire for you will never grow old, I proclaim.
I lay my head upon your bosom bare…
I feel the love that is in the air.
Your love intoxicates me like sweet wine divine,
As we so elegantly dine and I proclaim you are mine!

My Dearest Princess
By Thomas Joe Franks

When we first met, I saw the sunlight in your face.
I could not believe the beauty in which you were graced.
It was as if the sky opened up for the very first time
And the bright light of the sun did shine...
Bringing so much warmth that could not be confined.
Everything about you was illuminated.
Your gentleness, kindness, joy, sensitivity, passion, warmth,
And your compassion were all there for the world to see.
Every part of your face was elegant and exquisite.
Your eyes were pools filled with springs of water
And tender love.
Your lips were sensuous and just begged
To be touched and kissed.
It was at that very moment and for the very first time
That I realized that I had fallen in love with you...
And later to ask you to marry me.

It was as if every part of my body
Had been given a new lease on life.
No longer did I feel alone. I now felt joy, hope, and love.
I was so enamored and surprised
By your warmth and affection.
You seemed so interested in everything that I had to say.
You were never full of yourself.
You were content to hear all about me and my life.
You were encouraging...
As I spoke, you were always so interested.
I was very cautious about your feelings.
I did not want to move too quickly. I wanted to give you time.
You were gentle, accepting, and learned to trust me.

We have shared so many wonderful
And precious moments together.
I find that when I am alone, I miss you so much.
I find myself counting the hours and minutes...

When we will be together again!
Even our walks are wonderful...listening to the birds...
Seeing all the marvelous views...mountains...valleys.
Incredible!
I remember our first kiss.
How can I ever forget that moment in time?
I felt like I had found my very soul.
Now, I feel so renewed with awesome joy and love.
Thank you for that precious moment.
I now know that you feel the same way about me as I you.
We will spend more time together in just a few short days.
You have a very special place
In the recesses of my tender heart...
As we move forward with our hot
Passionate feelings for each other,
We will see even greater wonders and incredible things
Yet to come in our lives. I love you, Darling, yes I do!

Each Passing Moment
By Thomas Joe Franks

I miss you so desperately Karen G. Lovejoy.
I want to be near you and feel you ever so close to me.
I want to experience you.
I cannot fully explain it.
Even though, I am seldom "at a loss" for words,
No matter how I try to express myself in missing you...
The right words, logical words, rational words
Do not come easily.
This experience defies reason and deduction.
My heart... my little heart speaks to me
About you all the time.
You have looked into my soul...
And you know how I feel about you.
You are a special jewel...a sparkling perfect bright diamond.
You and God have given me hope, faith, and love...
Like a beacon in the night to a lonely ship.
I know it has only been a few days since I saw you,
But it feels like an eternity! Why?
Your absence has turned my life upside down. Why?
I want our lives to be woven together like the finest tapestry
Of all the known world...
The most exquisite embroidery of all time.
I see your smile.
I see your beautiful face.
I long to be with you each passing moment.
You make my heart feel as big as the earth itself! Why?
You have changed my darkest night into the noonday.
Only you can fill this empty space in my tender heart! Why?
Every day without you is another day without my
Princess. Why?
What am I to do? What am I to say?

Well, at least, since I met you, I'm not in a fog anymore.
And the consolation is: You will be in my arms again soon.
Let me attempt to explain it
The way an "artist" would explain it.
Missing you is like "doing a painting"...in drab colors.
However, being with you is like experiencing
Every stroke of the brush on the canvas
With bright illuminated colors.
The rainbow brush strokes seem
To just automatically come to life...and stand out.
To the multitudes who are looking on...
The artist experiences his dreams and visions
As he puts the finishing touches to his masterpiece.
Then...The sounds of your laughter are heard.
The smell of your perfume is in the air.
Your enveloping warm smile penetrates my deepest desire.
You have overwhelmed me with pure joy. Why?
My heart is racing. Now, I know how an artist feels.
Are you an artist? I think so. Please hurry to me. I miss you!

Karen, My Sweet Love (Part 1)

By Thomas Joe Franks

As I look into your eyes.
I see your beauty so sublime.
You are everything I have dream about.
You are and ever will be Karen, My Love!

I look deep into your emerald green eyes.
I see some of your past
And even a bit of your loneliness.
But most of all, I see such a wonderful delight.

I believe I understand you,
At least most of the time.
I want you to feel secure in my arms,
Without any pain in your gentle heart.

No more pain for you Baby,
No more apprehensions of the future.
We both have learned by experience
That a rainbow follows the rain!

Many questions have surfaced.
Many answers have been given.
We have become soul mates over the past years.
I will hold your hand forever, it is quite clear.

As I look into your eyes again,
I see that I am your good friend...
And your lover without end.
Our lives together, we will spend!

As the days pass, Karen My Love...
My passion for you grows more each day.

I feel incredibly excited each time...
That you tell me you love me on this mountain climb.

You have taken the disasters in my life
And turned them into happiness without strife.
I believe in you.
You have brought light to me in my darkest hour.

When I fell into your arms,
You received the key to my very soul.
I found celestial paradise extolled.
1000 years from now,
I will fall in love with you all over again!

Karen, My Sweet Love (Part 2)

By Thomas Joe Franks

Karen, My Love, You are my happiness.
Darling, you are more than a woman.
You breathe life to me.
You bring sweet memories of glee.

Hold me close to your heart.
We will never part.
Caress me tightly in your arms.
You are a lovely piece of art.

You are important to me.
Everything you do matters to me.
I think of us being together under the tall oak trees.
Together forever we will be.

It's so true...I Love You.
As I Look deeply into your green eyes,
I hear the sweet silence of your voice.
You whisper to me, "I Love You too."

I come closer to your lips.
I gently kiss you one more time.
Like it was our very first time.
Woman, I know that you will always be mine!

Words to Each Other
By Thomas Joe Franks

I woke up this morning feeling fine
Because I was lying next to you feeling so divine.
And you were holding me
And your head was resting gently on my shoulder.
You were whispering to me,
"I'm in love with you."
I'm in love with you.
So glad I found you…
I'm in love with you."

Remembering my dreams and rolling back the covers,
I began to get ready for the day ahead.
You looked at me in the mirror while I was shaving…
And gently said again, "I'm in love with you."
Before I leave, I say to you,
"Darling, I'm also in love with you.
You're the one I have chosen.
At times, our love is pure joy and other times,
It may be a little painful.
But through it all, it's always lovely to dance
With you in the rain."

Love is kissing in the rain.
Love is doing dishes late at night even with a migraine.
Love can be the art of compromise.
Love is more delightful than sweet wine.
I love you more today than I did yesterday!
Your kisses are sweeter than ruby red wine.
The fragrance of your perfume
Is so pleasing to my sense of smell.
Let me hear your sweet voice again…
And let me see your lovely face one more time.

My Love Is For All Seasons
By Thomas Joe Franks

I Love you Karen in the springtime when all is green and new.
I Love you in the summer when the sky is so blue.
I Love you in the autumn when the leaves are turning brown.
I Love you in the winter when the snow is falling down.

I Love you when I'm happy…and even when I'm sad.
I Love you when I'm good…or when I'm oh so bad.
I Love you when I'm tired…or when I am at rest.
I Love you when I'm feeling good…or even when I'm a pest.

I will Love you always Darling…in the rain or shining sun.
I will Love you always Darling…after all the time is done.
I will Love you always Darling…until all our life is through.
I will Love you always Darling…
And I will always be close to you.

Forever and a Day
By Thomas Joe Franks

I just want to say, I love you forever and a day!
That is always.
I dream of walking with you on the sand and bay.
We will walk together come what may...
We will be happy and gay...jubilant together.
You know what I mean.
Let's roll in the hay.
It's a good, good day.
We could sing the song of the Blue-Jay today.
We will be together soon in the Month of May.
Some may say, "Nay"...But I say "Yea"!
I have fallen in love with the Princess of the X-ray.
Soon you will be by my side to stay.
It's important for me to convey
Seven incredible words today...
"I love you...forever and a day!"

Happy Mother's Day to Karen
By Thomas Joe Franks

With Mother's Day approaching, I must tell you something.
I believe that you are a wonderful, incredible mother...
Because you not only love your children,
But you also show your love to them.
You have taught them values, principles, and respect.

You know I love red carnations, especially on Mother's Day.
I believe they signify the kind of sweetness
That you project on Mother's Day
And every day throughout the year.
A red carnation means that you are alive among the living.

A pink carnation conveys that you are far away...
And I believe you know
What a white carnation means...
However, you will be around
For another 50 years at least
You are so lovely and lively...Healthy and spirited at heart...
I love your affectionate and sexy smile.

I know you are a great mother...
You are also my incredible sweetheart.
Your laughter never seems to fade...You never seem to tire.
Your incredible love sets my soul on fire.
You are my desire in whom I admire!

This Sunday is your special day...
Hopefully, you will not have to cook.
Even though you are the greatest cook around...
It's your day to rest.
I am still a soldier boy, but If I were there, we'd roll in the hay.

Please have a Happy and Beautiful Mother's Day!

And oh, by the way... I bought a toupee!
Just kidding, Just kidding!
Oh, how much I do like to play.
For this Mother's Day, I send you a multitude
Of hugs and kisses...
You are such a lovely, sweet smelling bouquet.

As I sit here remembering the times we have shared…
The good times so numerous.
Our laughter so plentiful… Some do not appreciate
What they have until it's gone.
So I want you to know, in my plans for you…
You will not be alone.
I plan to walk with you hand in hand
Throughout the land that we have known.

Happy Mother's Day, Karen! You deserve the very best.
Do you understand how much I care?
I always want to be with you there.
I need you now more than ever.
I know in my heart that we will soon be together.
Then we will Talk and Talk...and Walk and Walk.

On every Lakeland sidewalk…
Love and laughter are in the air.
We have both waited so long for our special day,
So for now, have a sweet Mother's Day. I love you, Karen!

You Are the Spring in My Heart
By Thomas Joe Franks

I love the morning after the rain.
The quiet after the storm...
I love the dew on the roses,
The sun on my face...
And you...My Love...in my arms.
Take a look in the mirror, Baby.
What do you see?
I'll tell you what I see,
The most beautiful woman under heaven and on earth.
You Are the Spring in My Heart!

Don't change a thing.
I love you the way you are...
You are a precious jewel that sparkles even in the night!
The very first time I saw you,
I knew you were the one for me at first sight.
Never a question about it...
I never thought it was possible to care so much
For one person...
But each day that passes,
I miss you and want to feel your touch.

There's something so special about you,
That I've never found before.
Each day that passes, I find myself wanting you more.
To have you in my life,
Is like having honey on creamy, vanilla ice-cream...
Or maple syrup on Belgium waffles.
You make my life complete.
When I look at you, my heart skips a beat.
You are everything I ever wished for and more.
Now my dreams have come true.

You Are the Spring in my step and in my Heart.
My heart is filled with such love for you.
I know we'll never part.
My heart sings with harmony...
You are a delicate piece of art.
The heavens opened up the first day we met.
My love for you...I will always impart.
You are at the very top of my chart.
My Darling, I truly love you with all my soul and heart.
You have given me wonderful feelings right from the start!

I Feel You In My Arms Again
By Thomas Joe Franks

I love the way your hands softly caress my back.
You make me melt like butter in the Florida sun.
With your arms around me, my every nerve is tingling.
Why, you asked? Because of my need of you.

As you so gently wrap your arms around me...
And softly kiss my forehead,
You inevitably send chills down my spine again...
The anticipation drives me wild!

I can't help myself.
I softly kiss your ruby red lips,
And touch your hot body with such excitement.
I caress you and draw your body close to mine!

At this point, I am filled with incredible excitement,
And much anticipation.
Our hot hands roam over each other, while all the time,
Knowing we will experience flames of rapture and rhapsody.

As I Feel You In My Arms Again,
Our hearts begin pounding with much pleasure...
As our fingers press against such treasures.
Our bodies are now wide awake without measure.

Our passion increases...Our souls ignite.
We kiss each other passionately.
I look into your eyes and see the light...
And know that I have been to Heaven
And back with such delight.

Our Love Will Last
By Thomas Joe Franks

In some cases, love lasts a lifetime.
Unfortunately, others do not.
True love lasts forever.
When love is incredible, there is no greater emotion!
Darling, what I feel for you is unforgettable and so incredible.
Sometimes, love is like playing a piano...
First, you must learn to play by the rules.
But sometimes, you must forget the rules...
And play from your heart.
As I reach up to hold a star
And sit by a burning fire,
Being with you is my greatest desire!
You always bring me lots of smiles...
Regardless of our travels and a long highway of many miles.

We all want to fall in love.
Love makes us feel completely alive.
Our every sense is heightened...
Our every emotion is enlightened...
We feel as if we are flying into the heavens...
The memories that we treasure
Are ours for the rest of our lives!
Our relationship of love is solid.
Sometimes, a love relationship can be like the sand
That is held in our hand.
If we open our hands fully, the sand remains with us.
If we attempt to close our hands
And squeeze too tightly...
The sand trickles through our fingers.

Our love relationship is open and honest...
Filled with respect and freedom for each other.

Our love will remain intact. Why?
Because we are not too possessive or wound too tight.
Our love is full of acceptance...Truly loving you has brought
New meaning into my life! We are NOT perfect persons.
However, I have learned to love you
Not because you are a perfect person,
But by learning to see and love you
As an imperfect person lovingly!
Does this make any sense?
Loving you deeply gives me strength.
Being loved by you deeply gives me courage.
You have made me laugh again
Sometimes, love has no rhyme or reason.
It just is. Sometimes, the ones without reason
Last the longest.
We not only marry someone we can live with,
But we also marry the person who we cannot live without!

Spring is Here
By Thomas Joe Franks

Spring will be here before you know it.
I love Spring Time and I love Autumn.
They are my favorite seasons.
To spend the winter in Florida each year
Is a tremendous pleasure.
Some people's hearts are in San Francisco.
Mine is in Florida, especially in Central Florida.
A day without you, Karen, is boring, dull, uneventful,
Monotonous, unexciting, tiresome, irksome, tedious, dull,
And very fatiguing...Do you get my drift?
A day without you is like a day without sunshine.
I love you incredibly...As a Daisy in the Springtime.
You remind me of a cool refreshing spring of clear water
That quenches and extinguishes my desert thirst.

Emerald Eyes

By Thomas Joe Franks

When you entered into my life,
My whole world...as I knew it then...ceased to exist.
How could I ever have known that I would fall in love
So deeply and passionately...
With such a beautiful woman...
Who could make me feel so alive,
So peaceful, with so much energy?
From the first moment we kissed,
My heart and soul have belonged to you...
And yours to me! This is so awesome!

You have such emerald green eyes
Of tenderness and kindness...
Your long blonde hair a blowing in the wind...
And your elegance displayed in royal class.
You remind me of a beautiful garden...
Where roses, Easter lilies, and carnations grow.
Our love will never be too slow or ever grow too old.
Our love will continue to be fresh and crisp
As a daisy in the Spring.
And you will always be as beautiful as a pretty rosebud
Filled with fresh snow on a mountain top.
I love you now more than you will ever know!

Darling, Have I Told You Lately...?

By Thomas Joe Franks

Have I told you lately how important you are to me
And how you make me feel?
You are indeed such a nice and wholesome person.
I need to tell you that more often.
You are so "Special" to me!
You light up my life.
You make others feel so special as well.
You are always smiling!
Our Love is so real.
I am glad that you are sharing your life with me.
I am good with words,
But sometimes my words do not describe you
To the fullest...
Nor do they do you complete justice.
You're so fine and you're all mine!
Wonderful!
Without you, I would be missing out on so much.
I care about you incredibly. I love you.
Have I Told You Lately How Much I Love You...?

Our Journey Together...You & I
By Thomas Joe Franks

As we travel down the road of life,
We follow with our two hearts together.
We keep our dreams in front of us.
We know the direction that we are going.
We have learned to notice the road signs along the way.
We KNOW who we are and where we are going.
The road under construction will not slow us down.
We have learned from our mistakes.
The road may have many curves...So what...
We will NOT be afraid.
We will arrive at our destination without delay!

Sometimes, we must slow down and proceed with caution.
We refuse to be distracted by Nay Sayers and tailgaters.
We are in the driver's seat...
We will be happy because we choose to be happy.
As we travel the open road at our own casual speed,
Our destination is always in our minds, thoughts, and spirits.
Occasionally, we do ask for directions.
One-way streets do not cause us concern
Because we KNOW there is only one direction to go...
Forward.
As we travel down the friendly pathway of Love,
We know that this adventure will lead us to our destiny!

As You Know
By Thomas Joe Franks

AS YOU KNOW,
I LOVE YOU SO
AS YOU ALSO KNOW,
I NEED YOU DESPERATELY.
AS YOU ADDITIONALLY KNOW,
I CARE DEEPLY FOR YOU.
AS YOU INDEED KNOW,
I MISS YOU INCREDIBLY.

AS YOU KNOW ALWAYS,
I WANT YOU.
AS YOU KNOW FOR CERTAIN,
I WANT TO HOLD YOU IN MY ARMS AGAIN.
AS YOU KNOW, I KNOW
THAT WE WERE MADE FOR EACH OTHER.
I KNOW. WE KNOW. EVERYONE KNOWS…
THAT WE ARE "IN LOVE" FOREVER!

Speaking of Dreams (Part 1)
By Thomas Joe Franks

As I began to dream,
I finally found myself.
I was in your arms with
My head resting gently
Upon your shoulder.
We were traveling somewhere
Just enjoying the solitude
Of one another.
We were in my black Mercedes
Taking it slow and easy!

We stopped at several places
Along the way.
I soon found myself
In your warm embrace.
I closed my eyes in peaceful sleep!
The moments we had together
In the dream were splendid and wonderful.
My heart was filled to overflowing.
I turned to you and said softly,
I love you incredibly.

As you responded passionately,
We met one another with lips of fire.
Our souls inwardly burned
With love and incredible emotion.
This dream was so real and vivid with life!
Soon, I realized that it was time to go.
I did not want to leave,
But this dream demanded it.
I wanted to share at least another moment with you
And look into your beautiful green eyes again!

We looked at each other
Without saying a word...
Knowing that we would meet again
In another passionate dream...
Another time, another place.
Our thoughts we dared not speak,
Knowing the words from our hearts
Would not be sufficient to prolong the dream.
We looked into the eyes of the other...
Knowing that we would wake up alone!

Speaking of Dreams (Part 2)
By Thomas Joe Franks

We enjoyed the moment together.
We were fascinated once again.
We said, "I love you" to the other.
We knew we would be back
Because this dream would be continued!
As we departed,
You spoke ever so softly and quietly,
Almost in a whisper.
I heard you say once again,
"I love you."

My heart leaped…Your words covered me.
They sank into my heart…Sort of like warm maple syrup
Being poured on fresh, hot, Belgium waffles.
The joy of it all…We dared to love.
We dared to share….We dared to feel.
We dared to show our feelings…The dream was perfect.
The dream was complete.
The dream was fulfilling.
The dream was innocent.
The dream ended!

Autumn 2004...My Sweet Lover Karen

By Thomas Joe Franks

The leaves are turning.
The weather is getting cooler.
The days are getting shorter.
Over two years ago, you gave my life a new start.
My weaknesses...you turned into strengths.
You have turned my bad times into good times.
With you, the difficult moments
Have been easier to go through.
You have turned my "down times" into "good times"!

Your sweet ruby red lips have kissed away my tears.
Every time I needed you,
You were there by my side.
You have taught me to be strong,
And to be calmer...and to slow down...at least while eating!
You showed me how to let go...and move forward.
Old memories have been left behind.
We now make plans together for the future
As our love is refined!

Every autumn gives ways to the winter,
Sometimes snow...sometimes rain.
You have taught my heart to forgive even more.
And to love more passionately.
Through this journey, you have been with me
Every step of the way.
You have never complained, even when it rained.
For your beauty and love, you have not asked
For anything in return.
You are my best friend, lover, companion,
Advisor, and faithful wife.

You do not judge me in anyway…
Even while on the highways.
You are so caring, honest, and fun to be with.
Your kisses are sweeter than red Australian wine.
You have loved me more with the passing of time.
Ever since we met, our love has grown a little each day!
When we married, we vowed, to let
Nothing on this earth break us apart.
You are indeed the apple of my heart!

The longer I am with you…
The more I feel that we were destined to be together.
I love you more than mere words could ever say.
My heart feels so light and full because
You are such a sweet bouquet!
We are happy… delightful… and blessed
With the love of each other.
What else matters? I love you! Happy Autumn 2004.

Your Passionate Lover
By Thomas Joe Franks

Once upon a time,
There lived a beautiful woman…
With whom I fell in love.
I knew that I would go anywhere
In the whole wide world to be with this angelic being!
I'd cross the deepest ocean if need be,
I'd go to the highest mountain if necessary,
I'd cross any desert if required.
Suddenly, the love gates opened!
Passion was at our door.
Our hearts wanted more.
This, we could not ignore!

The candles were brightly burning.
A wonderful sweet, aromatic fragrance was in the air.
We were so close to one another.
The temperature suddenly changed in the room…
From cool to warm to hot.
Your incredible green eyes and hot body
Got my undivided attention!
The evening was young.
The moon was bright.
Our lips were hot.
Passion and love were closer than before!
Discovering your soft touch galore…
Was far better than being in a chocolate store!

That night, I became your passionate lover.
Now, I feel like I'm in flowers of clover.
My passion for you boils over.
I'm so in love with such a beautiful woman!

You have stolen my tender heart,
I know that we will never part.
Our passion has been steamy from the very start.
Our lives have purpose and meaning to impart.
The sound of laughter from your eyes...
Is much better than a million dollar prize!
Your soft, sexy whispers make my temperature rise...
Which often lead to cries, sounds of passion, and sighs!

Do You Ever Cross My Mind?
Happy Second Wedding Anniversary
To Karen Gwyn Franks
By Thomas Joe Franks

Do you ever cross my mind?
Funny question! All the time…
When I think of you, I wish we could go back in time…
And make Sweet memories so sublime.
Do you ever cross my mind!

Do you ever cross my mind?
Sometimes, in the middle of the night…
Even in my dreams, I see us toasting
With delicious ruby red wine,
And making memories so passionately defined!
I see you as a woman in silk with emerald green eyes…
Incredibly refined.

What about the feelings when you cross my mind?
They remind me of a candlelight dinner…
For two with heavenly food so divine…
Dancing until 2 AM under the bright neon signs.
Hello! Do you ever cross my mind!

Sometimes, I wish that we could go back in time…
Our lives would be re-designed.
I see us taking a river boat cruise down the River Rhein
And enjoying the medieval castles under
The romantic German sunshine.
I promise to be gentle and hold you close
To this passionate heart of mine!

As my Bride and green eyed Blonde,
Do you ever cross my mind? Hello!
During the past two years of marriage,
You have forever crossed my mind!
You have helped me to stay in line...
And have brought me calmness and daily warm sunshine!

Warm Ruby Red Lips
By Thomas Joe Franks

My warm ruby lips are drawn to your warm ruby red lips,
Intoxicating like old wine or
Like juicy red grapes.
Our kisses are long and wet and delicious
Our passionate desires
Are from one heart to the other.
Our kissing is submerged in an ocean of pleasures.
The drummer of love thunders.
We are excited from within!
Our hands caress each other.
Your body is like the sculptor of a goddess of clay.
Our love is intertwined ...man and woman immersed in love.
It's like sailing on clouds
In the spring sunshine.

Our streams of passions go untamed...
Like a man and woman snowed in...
Or caught up to the third heaven.
I kiss you on your forehead
And later on your warm ruby lips.
We make love.
You are the sweetest woman in the world!
You make me feel so good inside.
You are with me.
You are an absolute angel.
You mean the world to me!
Everything that you do seems so right for me.
I want to hold you tight, especially at night.
The world knows about our love.
Kiss me one more time with your ruby red lips.

Your sweet kisses are real.
They are straight from your heart.
I longed for this day...
When I could share my love with
The woman of my dreams!
When you are by my side,
I am cool, calm, and collected.
I now leave you with a tender, gentle kiss.
You are always in my heart.
Our kisses will never part!

You Are Always In My Thoughts and Dreams

By Thomas Joe Franks

The other night as you lay calmly by my side,
To myself, I had to confide
That our love, we could not hide.
I think of you often like all the time,
Especially, when the birds sing and the clock chimes.
Today, when I awoke, I missed you in my strong arms.
I missed your elegant green eyes
And your magnificent charm!

We will be together again soon,
Our passion is as hot as the sun at noon.
As we celebrate our love,
The fleeting moments become a little heaven from above.
But it's the nights that give me pain,
Because your love and charm are like the gentle rain.
I miss you because you are sweeter
Than all the Florida sugarcane.

You have filled the empty spaces in my heart,
Your eyes have told me that we will never part.
Your sexy voice is sweet and like a cherry tart.
You have touched my heart with your warmth and kindness.
We laughed, talked, and played again and again!
This morning, I opened my eyes to the dark silent night,
I see you so often in my sweet dreams delight!

It's All About Us
By Thomas Joe Franks

My Darling, do not imagine,
As you write more lines in your journal...
That I have been trespassing on your heart.
It's not your imagination. I have.
Hopefully, I have written my love on your heart.
I always long to write you love letters,
Especially when we're apart.
It's all about us! Why?
I wish I knew.
I seem to breathe you. I seem to hear you.
I seem to feel you. It's all about you.
It's all about us. What is our destiny?
Why are we here?
Is it not to love one another passionately
And live our lives incredibly together?
I have seen the valley. I have seen the mountain top.
Today, as we embark on this adventuresome journey,
We talk. We walk. We love.
We gaze into each other's eyes in the candle light.
Flowers are on the table.
From dusk till dawn,
We hug. We dance. We kiss.
We enjoy each other's company.
Our colorful garden of life is full and enchanting.
We get up. We drink the aromatic Arabian hot coffee.
You write some more in your journal.
Your pen gets low on ink,
But you continue to write.
You feel safe. And you should.
You're with me.
The clock continues to tick.

Why are we here? What is our destiny?
To love each other...
To care...
To respect...
To honor...
To cherish...One another.
It's all about us!
I love you.

Love is the Most Important Feeling
By Thomas Joe Franks

Karen, since meeting you, I know that Love is the
Most Important Feeling that one can experience.
I used to think that love was only real in the movies...
I used to think that I did not need anyone
Because I felt so strong and independent.
But now, my attitude about love and care and needing
Someone has changed a lot...somewhat.
Now, our relationship has become passionate,
Yet transparent.
We want to tell the world that something is so good...
So wonderful.
We are in love!
I am not afraid to admit that love is the most important feeling
One can experience...
And I want to thank you for causing me to be
Honest with myself and others.
It is just impossible to capture in words
My feelings for you... impossible!
All I can tell you is: My feelings are the strongest feelings
That I have ever had about anything or any person.
Yet, sometimes, when I try to convey my love to you,
My words do not even begin to touch
The depths of my feelings.
Although I cannot explain the essence
Of these phenomenal feelings,
I can tell you what I feel like when I am with you.
I feel like a butterfly blowing in the wind
Under blue cloudless skies.
Henceforth, when I am with you, I feel like a flower...
Opening up my petals of life to you.
Henceforth, when I am with you,

I feel like the ocean waves crashing
Strongly against the shoreline.
Henceforth, When I am with you, it is as if I am a rainbow
Proudly showing my colors.
Henceforth, when I am with you, it is as if everything
That is beautiful surrounds us.
This is just a very small part of how
Wonderful I feel...when I am with you.
Our love is deep, all-encompassing, strong, stable, and
Eternal. I love you more than mere words or mere gestures.
I never thought I would find this kind of love.
You are indeed the right person for me to love.
My Love for You has now become
The most important part of my life.
Our love will last and become even more beautiful.
Please Note: Always know that I love you
More than anything else on Planet Earth.

You Are My Sweet Angel Karen
By Thomas Joe Franks

Every day all around us,
Angels are helping us.
They bring us smiles, hope, and happiness.
Angels help us build bridges...not walls.
They help us to get along with our fellowman.
They don't have hidden agendas
Or hide the truth from us.
They understand what we are going through.
If we are hurting, they try to help us.
Angels understand our difficulties and doubts.
Angels bring us inner beauty.
Angels do not hold things against us;
However, they do hold us up!
They hold our hands many times in life.
They walk beside us and help guide us.
They support us in doing the right thing...
Even though at times, it may be difficult!
Angels make us feel good about ourselves.
They motivate us.
They love us.
They make us feel "special and needed".
A few months ago,
I came across an angel like this.
She is so beautiful.
She is so kind to me...not mean to me!
She has my best interest at heart and in her mind.
She gives me such a "high" in living.
She makes me feel so special.
What is her name?
Her name is Karen.
Karen is my Sweet Angel...
And I love her incredibly!

What Do I See When I look At You?
By Thomas Joe Franks

I see a gorgeous, beautiful woman...
Blossoming forth as a desert rose.
You remind me of the early rain...
On the picturesque plain in romantic Spain.
You are continuing to grow...
Like a rose petal touched by a raindrop on a plateau!

I see more than a beautiful woman.
I see an individual who is free to think,
Free to make decisions on her own.
She doesn't need someone telling her what to do,
Even though I think she truly needs me
Through and through!
Regardless, she is free from despair, dismay, and disarray!

I see an elegant, stunning woman...
Free from guilt and shame,
Who has become my beau and flame.
I see a woman discovering her true identity and beauty!
She is surrounded by rays of sunshine and splendor.
Each new day brings a brand new bouquet so tender!

Her life, her beauty, her slender body...
Do not fog her vision or make her vain.
What do I see?
I see a woman who is beautiful and young at heart
In her reign, who has let go of the old...
And is now thinking of new dreams and horizons
Bold to behold!

My Love for You (Karen)
By Thomas Joe Franks

Your beautiful blonde hair...
The way it floats in the air,
Your smile...The way it makes me feel so alive.
As do your luscious red lips...And those wonderful hips...
And your breasts that are like clusters of grapes.
Your green eyes are always so aglow,
You could be the star of any Broadway Show!

Your cheerful rose cheeks...
I can hardly speak.
Your beauty
Is truly like no other...no other. Period.
That's why I want you...I need you.
And no other.
I seek your love more than any red wine.

What is it about you...
That makes my stomach turn?
My heart beat faster?
My blood pressure go high?
Is it your beautiful smile?
Your sexy burgundy lips?
How beautiful you are my Darling!

Is it the sweetness of your voice?
Your radiant and beautiful smile?
The way you walk?
The way you talk?
Is it the way I see you in the sunset?
Or is it our passion and love when we are alone?
You are mine and I am yours.

We have talked and we have laughed.
We have dreams of being together.
You and I are meant to be…
You will have to agree.
We both have so much to give.
And many years to live. I love you.
My Darling…Sweet Darling, rendezvous with me.

My Light Haired Maiden
By THOMAS JOE FRANKS

You are my light haired maiden
That has forever invaded the estate of my mind.
Without hesitating or awaiting,
I have found you to be ever so kind.
My heart has been captivated
And even fascinated by your design.

If I were an earthly king with a throne,
I would abdicate today
In order to spend just one moment with you alone.
Never would I vacillate or delay,
But would sound the alarm over the megaphone
That you are "My Light Haired Maiden"
Like a Fragrant Bouquet.

My Best Friend Karen
By Thomas Joe Franks

Our friendship is Special and Beautiful.
Our unique friendship is also intimate.
I can say that Karen is truly my best friend
Because I know that she is the one person
In whom I can always confide without being condemned
Or fear retribution.
My joys are her joys.
My pains are her pains.
My goals and aspirations
Are encouraged by this wonderful being.
I believe that a friend is a special gift that you give yourself.
In 2003, I gave myself a special gift…
Worth more than the whole world.
I gave myself Karen Gwyn.
She is not the type of gift that walks in front of me
Or who walks behind me.
She is my friend. She walks with me and beside me.

Your Beautiful Emerald Green Eyes (Part 1)
By Thomas Joe Franks

As I looked into your beautiful emerald eyes,
I could see that you were indeed a "rare find"!
I had dreamed about you so many times,
But now, you were far more beautiful than I had imagined.
Even though, we have only known each other a short time...
It seems like a lifetime.

As I looked into your beautiful emerald green eyes,
I could see deep into your very soul.
My hand touched your hand...
And I decided to never let go! Hello!
As I look back, I am so amazed at how fast the time has gone.
I am so happy I know that we will never again be alone!

As I looked into your beautiful emerald green eyes,
I could now see how much we have changed
Over the past few months.
We have grown together...in love, happiness, and joy.
You have become the "apple of my eye"...
The incredible woman who loves me dearly!
Words almost fail me at this point,
But my passionate response is,
"Darling, I will love you forever"!

Now, as I look into your beautiful emerald green eyes,
I asked, "Where has the time gone?"
"Where have the days gone?"
We have talked for hours and hours.
We simply enjoy the other.
These moments will never end!

As I look into your beautiful emerald green eyes,
I now see that our time has come.
You wrap your arms of love around me.
I feel so alive, a little nervous...and so incredibly excited.
A new beginning has occurred.
Turn to me...hug me...kiss me...never let me go!

Your Beautiful Emerald Green Eyes (Part 2)

By Thomas Joe Franks

As I look into your beautiful emerald green eyes,
I see your incredible beauty.
I want to share my life with you!
You are the right person.
This is a beautiful day indeed!
The excitement overwhelms me!

As I look into your beautiful emerald green eyes,
I see your love for me.
We have something so special and so incredible
And so unforgettable!
I'll spend my life with you...caring for you...nurturing you.
This is only the beginning.
Each day will be special with you...I love you!

As I look into your beautiful emerald green eyes,
I know that good things will come to us. Life is good!
I now hold you in my arms and promise
To be there for you at all times.
We will share our laughter, smiles,
And even our struggles together.
I will hold you during our triumphs, our joys,
And even our disappointments!
We both will grow...Our moments together will never end!

My Princess Karen Gwyn
By Thomas Joe Franks

It seems like an eternity since I last saw you.
I love the sparkle in your emerald green eyes.
I love your giggle and laugh.
You have taken my world by storm.
You are such an innocent and lovely Princess galore.
You have bonded with my soul and more.
One day, we will be inseparable...Oh yes!
No more leaving you ever.
My thoughts and desires are with you now
In my tender heart.
I am yours.
Soon, our days will be filled with such delight.
As I have told you, everything will be all right!
As I look back on my childhood and light tragedies,
I wish I would have known you back then.
But the important thing is...I know you now!
You will soon be by my side.
I will take you by the hand and look into your eyes...And say
Those tender words that you love to hear:
"I Love You forever and always!"
Even though now we are far away from each other,
When I close my eyes, you are so near!
My heart sees you
Even though the weather is sometimes stormy,
As I think of you... There is no room
For storm clouds to gather
Around me...no time for gloom!
I want to look into your emerald eyes again.
My eyes miss your beauty so close.
My tender heart misses your sweet small voice.

My memories are strong and sure,
As I see the sparkle in your eyes.
No shadows are near...just your angelic Princess face and
Bright clear skies!

Delicious Love
By Thomas Joe Franks

It seems like only yesterday.
We met for the very first time.
How the sweetness lingers in my mind.
You are so delightful and sweet.
The gentle cool breeze of spring was soon to follow.
I had no hair to blow in the wind,
But yours was soft and silky...I grinned.
The sun was bright that first day.
Your red convertible was comfortable and sporty.
You were and are such a joy to be with...
You made me laugh...And I made you smile.
The birds were flying high
As their wings stretched toward heaven.
The warmth in your smile
And the sparkle in your eyes made
Me realize what I had missed for a long, long time.
We both experienced much comfort in the newness
And freshness that still lingers today with passion.
Our words have become easy between us.
I now realize that I was falling in love
For the last time on that special day.
Delicious is our love!

You Have Captured My Heart
By Thomas Joe Franks

Karen, my Love, you have captured my tender heart.
You did so with such a brief encounter in part.
You looked at me as if you were on fire.
We both had the feeling of romance and love acquired.
You have blended so perfectly in your exquisite attire.
Into my life... from head to toe
You have become my high tower.
I had previously looked elsewhere...
Even at a French chateau.
But my eyes just wouldn't let you go.
You were sweeter and exquisite to me...
Better than any red Bordeaux.
At last, I'm in front of you,
The woman of such splendor aglow...
With such treasure glistening from the skies,
Showing your graceful elegance and incredible smile...
With your twinkling emerald green eyes.
I have tasted your beauty
And have seen your beautiful life style.
What a wonderful, wonderful feeling so deliberately agile.
The feeling of such a wonderful sensation...so worthwhile.
And so seductively appealing to my profile.
My Love, we have something so incredibly special,
I am getting to know
That I could get lost in this lovely feeling and tempo.
Why? Because you have captured my heart
With your passionate glow!

Best Of Friends With Karen Lovejoy
By Thomas Joe Franks

How was your day today?
It was like a sunny day in May.
I was able to help someone along the way.
I gave them hope and told them that life can be fun,
And that the battles of life could be won
Through Jesus Christ, the Holy One!

And how was your day today?
It was almost as marvelous as being with you
In a small cafe.
I spoke a word of encouragement
To someone in dismay.
The person was filled with hurts, pains
And thoughts of the past.
After we had prayed, he felt peace at last.
Now, his future looks bright with a heavenly forecast!

The above examples are deeds we have shared together.
I am so fortunate to have a friend like Karen
Who truly cares
And spreads cheer, comfort, and love everywhere.
I can't imagine Karen going through a day
Without stopping to help
Someone in disarray… And giving them
A rainbow of sunshine as a bouquet.
I love her. She is my BEST FRIEND!

The Green Eyed Lady (Part 1)
By Thomas Joe Franks

There she stood with a bright eyed smile
That reminded me of spring on a clear, crisp day.
Was she looking at me or was she looking at him
As she sang an old familiar hymn?

The air seemed to flow through her bright blonde curls
As her green eyes seemed to twinkle and sparkle.
Joy was evidenced by her cheery countenance
Of radiant glory
And suddenly I knew that I would have to know
More about her story

I felt drawn by an outside force to investigate further this
Wonderful and fathomless feeling.
Was this a myth or musical beauty?
Was this a dream or vision of a heavenly angel?

My heart pondered as I wondered within my spirit
If she would be a special part of my life.
Would life truly become a reality and testimony
With this Green Eyed Lady in HOLY Matrimony?

Again, my heart started to beat with excitement as I began
My inquiries about this earthly creation of pure joy.
She has such a heavenly fluorescent face
Which is not a ploy.
Was she already "spoken for"
Somewhere in the marketplace?

Did she in fact belong to another
And would she in fact talk to

This lonely Knight dressed in armor...
Whose soul used to be less than white?
I presupposed and called for another meeting
And had some wonderful conversation after the greeting.

Little did I know that this Green Eyed Lady
Whom I wished would be Waiting had done her own Investigating.
Now she knew all about this chivalrous knight
Who looked like a hood and gangster type.

I arrived in my over-sized chariot
Which had the speed of Jehu the Daring.
What would be the anxious outcome of this Knight
Who looked as if he had come
From Sherwood Forest after a fight?

The Green Eyed Lady, would she be waiting
To help heal my wounded spirit?
Time passed ever so slowly, but suddenly there we stood
Face to face as only lovers could.

The Green Eyed Lady (Part 2)
By Thomas Joe Franks

Her face had a light tan and her eyes
Were deep, deep emerald green...
Which reminded me of a cool, clear, refreshing pool or spring,
Not an ordinary spring,
But one fed from a bed of mountain stones
On a hot summer's day...near a valley of aromatic pine cones.

A bit shy, my words came forth with tenderness
And the question was asked.
Would she share a ride with me
In my fiery chariot and spend some time
With this Knight who thought she was a brilliant emerald?

Would she go to the top of the world with this Knight
Who had seen so many wars
And had lost a few along the way?
Now he was on the mend
And awaiting her decision to descend.

An eternity passed it seemed,
But finally this Princess responded
Ever so softly with quiet words of harmony.
This wonderful Green Eyed Lady
With a smile from curl to curl,
Finally said, "Yes, you can take me to the moon and back."

The hours came and went ever so slowly.
The hours seemed like days and the days like weeks.
But finally that great day and hour of our third meeting
Became a reality and our time together was so entreating.

As I sped off like a football player from Clemson,
With the speed of an antelope, I was soon at her castle.
As I arrived in my black chariot,
She was standing tall inside by the window
Of the castle door.

I was greeted by a couple of distinctive people.
Within moments, a lovely creation
Of Beauty entered the room.
All of my thoughts and dreams changed
From the Feudal System
To the Modernistic times
Of radical festivities and gala jubilee.

Dressed in green, she was more beautiful
Than all the pearls of the sea.
The Green Eyed Lady had long, blonde, wavy hair.
Her slender legs and bosom breasts
Caught my eye immediately.
I pinched myself under the armor that I was wearing.

The Green Eyed Lady (Part 3)
By Thomas Joe Franks

With a twinkle in my eye, I thought to myself aloud,
"What a lovely creation of Beauty to behold under any bright cloud."
Her eyes were emerald green and sparkling
As the stars on a full moon
Ever so bright, exhilarating, and lively with excitement.

We exchanged amenities and I assisted her
Into my fiery chariot and
We were off to another part of the World.
On the journey, I listened; she talked.
She loved people. She laughed a lot.
Her smile never left her face.
She was nice and lovely and I was exhilarated.

Could this be a lasting friendship?
Could this be the woman and Princess in my life?
Would I always believe in this Green Eyed Lady of Beauty?
I certainly desired to give it a whirl. After all, "It's my duty."

Soon we arrived at our destination…Top of the Moon.
We were escorted in a hospitable and gracious manner
To a table set for a king and his queen.
She talked. I listened. I again thought I was sixteen.

We looked at the informative menu
And began a long discussion.
Would it be Prime Rib, Leg of Lamb,
Filet of Sole, or Would it be

Filet Mignon cut from the choicest,
Succulent, beef tenderloin?
Beautiful night...I would wait on the Princess to enjoin.

The Green Eyed Lady began to peruse the finest cuisine
That silver and gold could possibly buy...
And within a few moments,
A large warm smile broke the silence from her lovely face.
She would have fillet mignon
With a baked potato on the side.

Contrary to my delicate taste buds,
I did not want her to know
That I was not a fine discriminatory connoisseur,
With the finest appreciation of exquisite foods.
Therefore, I ordered the steak too,
Like a Knight from Timbuktu.

Her emerald eyes were like pure wells
Of sparkling, clean, refreshing water.
We chatted with small talk in the beginning,
But before long, things began to happen in a wonderful way.
I suddenly knew that this beautiful creation
Would be mine someday.

The Green Eyed Lady (Part 4)
By Thomas Joe Franks

We ate, we laughed, we drank, we talked.
We were lavishly entertained with love songs
That seemed to unify
Our spirits as we looked at each other aflame...
Her green dress and my dark suit of armor reclaimed.

This night was a night that this Knight will always remember.
I remember talking to her as if we had known
Each other for a long time.
I continued to think that this Green Eyed Lady
Would some day
Be a greater part of my life to stay.

MEMORIES, SWEET MEMORIES are ever so sweet
When you find peace of
Mind and what you have been looking for,
Such a long, long time.
Today, this SWEET MEMORY (the Green Eyed Lady)
Has become a Reality
In my life on a daily basis
And it's truly ADVENTURESOME and delightful.

PS: Life continues and we have now been married (happily)
For over sixteen years...

My Darling Karen
By Thomas Joe Franks

You have turned my life upside down.
I love you incredibly.
And you know in your heart that I so desperately need you.
Our love will mend our lives together forever.
You have gone thru a lot in your lifetime.
If you only knew how much I wanted you...
If you only knew how much I love you...
If you only knew how much I needed you...
If you only knew how much I care for you...
If you only knew how much I dream about you...
If you only knew how much I plan with you...
If you only knew how much I think of you…
If you only knew how much I desire to be near you...
You would NEVER again be lonely, afraid, or apprehensive...
You would NEVER again walk alone or feel sad again.
You would NEVER again be without me
To love, cherish, and adore you!
I know you love me...as I love you.
I know you want to be with me.
To start your life over with me.
To begin a future with me.
To plan our golden years together.
To provide a good and healthy future.
You know I love you immensely...and incredibly.
Loving you is the easiest thing that I have ever done!

The Season of Christmas with Family and Friends
By Thomas Joe Franks

The season of Christmas is the most wonderful time of year,
Celebrating with family and friends with joy and cheer...
Sharing gifts...and singing carols so dear!
This is our first Christmas together
As husband and wife!
You are my special gift so full of life.
More than any other...
You have already given me so much good advice.

The season of Christmas is the most wonderful time of year!
You are my favorite green-eyed blonde, friend, and such
a dear.
You have given me so much love!
You have shared your heart with me...
Closer than two mourning doves.
As I look upon the stars above,
I know that my Christmas wish has come true.
Your love, care, friendship rule.
When I'm with you, I feel so cool.

The season of Christmas is the most wonderful time of year!
The best lies ahead.
Merry Christmas to You, my love.
When I kiss you under the mistletoe,
Your fire and the spirit of Christmas light up my soul.
Your soft, gentle hands rubbing my bald head
Bring warmth, love, and tenderness that fills the air.
I move closer to you without any despair about hair!

The season of Christmas is the most wonderful time of year,
Especially when I hold you tightly...
Running my fingers through your hair.
Lovingly, passionately, and softly
I caress your soft and beautiful body.
Your hands slowly move to my neck and hairless head.
Our eyes lightly close as we touch our lips.
Our feelings cannot be expressed by mere words
Because our love goes as deep as nature will permit.
I then realize you are the one, my sweet love,
Whom I have dreamed about all my life.

With just one sweet and loving kiss,
You showed me that I could love again.
I know this Holiday is like a shining star,
For God in Heaven, brought you to me from afar.
You are such a lovely angel and Princess,
Who has brought me words of joy and happiness...
I love you!
Tonight, under the mistletoe, let us never forget...
That the Christmas season is such a wonderful time of year!

You Are God's Special Gift To Me!
By Thomas Joe Franks

You are a very SPECIAL Gift...
That the world can truly see.
The reason you are so SPECIAL is...
You were sent from God to me!

Whenever you feel unappreciated or lonely,
Just remember there is someone who thinks
You're the "one and only".
You remind me of fine, precious, and aromatic perfume...
Made from fresh, red rose petals in full bloom!

I promise you...You will never be taken for granted
Because you are an eternal gift in my heart deeply planted.
From the very beginning of time,
God knew that one day, you'd be mine!

I love you because you speak from your heart.
To me, you are sweet music and an incredible work of art.
You have caused me to truly love you
And feel young again.
Now, my heart is truly in an enchanted tailspin!

Life Is Good
By Thomas Joe Franks

We have started our journey together.
Life is good!
It is so wonderful to have found a woman
Who loves me as much as I love her.
I can't wait to see what our future holds.
I am extremely excited to have such a person in my life
In whom I cherish each and every day.
Loving you fills me with great pleasure.

We had been married only a short time
As you continued to sweep my heart away.
Somehow, I knew we would be good together.
Day after day my love for you has grown stronger.
We have had so many experiences already...
We will certainly have many more to come.
We have shared so much and had so much fun.
Our summer days have been beautiful and hot under the sun.

You have made me one happy man. My life has changed.
I love you more now than I ever have in the past.
Every day you make my heart tick a little faster.
I love to feel your tender touch and tender kisses...
And of course your sweet lips and impeccable breasts.
Every day that goes by...with you in my arms...
Makes me feel so good inside. Life is good.
Every day that goes by I love you more and more.

I appreciate you more each passing day!
I am your tender and gentle husband to stay.
You are my sweet and calm wife. You are so lovely and kind.
You are such a tremendous part of my life and ever so fine.

I will hold you in my arms and in my heart forever.
We have such fond memories to share!
I feel like I have been walking on air.
You are my best friend and passionate lover
Who truly cares.

I appreciate you being there and listening to me complain
When my day isn't going just right...or when I am in traffic.
You seem to know what to say to calm me down.
I want you to always know that I will be there for you too...
To lean on...when you need to lean on me.
Memories... we will share. Feelings...we will care.
Our love...will always have class and style...
And a flair for excitement and passion worthwhile.

Love and Care
By Thomas Joe Franks

For me "Love & Care" mean something different,
Especially for a VIP who loves me so.
Yes, I have many friends and family members…
Deep within the recesses of my heart.
In the past, it has been good to share with them often…
And to get some great advice or a listening and hearing ear.
I need to think things through occasionally.
And during those times, I do not want to be alone
While thinking on so many important issues!

At times, I must confront my deepest feelings
Before they become a warehouse of shattered dreams,
Unfulfilled hopes, or disillusioned aspirations.
This is where true "love and caring"
Comes into the big picture.
A family member may reaffirm the thoughts of my heart
And truly want what is best for me and what is to be.
Yet, Karen is that special passionate friend
Who has discovered a loving way into my heart…
In which I know we will never part.

What do I do? What do I say?
Do I allow this "Princess" person to see…
To feel, to share, to read my mind so passionately?
Or do I dispose of all my uncertainty
And all the emotions that I have ignored…
For such a long, long time?
Or do I allow this woman to be a part of my new perspective
That quietly settles down in the ramparts of my heart?
"Love and Care" are the ingredients of a long life to impart.

You are an Elegant Woman of Color
By Thomas Joe Franks

During the 60s, the bright golden, yellow days
Of your youth eventually
Faded into the 70s of growing responsibilities
Of green pastures for your family.
The night was soon falling and sometimes,
It was pitch black right before dawn.
Nonetheless, you experienced a multitude
Of colors for your life
As you entered the prosperous 80s...Of the sands of time!

The late red sunsets, the early morning blue skies,
The summer rainbows all made
An incredible contribution to you in the 90s.
Now, the 21st century is here.
You are now so warm...Your ruby red lips are so soft
As I look into your emerald green eyes!

Your soft, surging blonde hair waves to me in the sunlight.
There seems to be a fiery orange glow around you
As I take you into my loving arms.
Your heart to my heart will never be blue again...
Your days of "blue" are now over!

You are my childhood dream come true.
You remind me of a tall oak tree in the autumn...
Full of so many yellow, brown, golden, rich lavender,
And deep orange leaves!
You are indeed an Elegant Woman of Color.
You have brightened my life a thousand fold...
I love you, my Darling Karen!

I asked, "Where has the time gone?"
"Where have the days gone?"
We have talked for hours and hours.
We simply enjoy the other.
These moments will never end my woman of color.

Our Love Feels So Right
By Thomas Joe Franks

As I watched you out of the corner of my eye,
I turned my head to soak in your beauty!
I must have stared for several minutes,
Fascinated by your elegance, grace, and charm.
I wanted so desperately to kiss your soft, slender hand.
I watched your sweet lips form a smile.
You greeted me with soft sweet words of welcome.
Your smile melted my tender heart.
The glow on your beautiful face captured my mind.
Your bright, green emerald eyes arrested my soul.

Your smile placed me at a disadvantage
Because I was so vulnerable to your womanhood.
Smiles in the past paled in comparison to your smile.
When you laughed, I beamed with excitement!
We talked for a long time together.
I know that you have great abilities as an artist,
Visionary, romantic thinker, mother, and liberated woman.
You are a giver...You want to help people.
Now, I have fallen in love with you.
I now believe in love again!

I want to walk and talk with you for the next 50 years.
In spring, simmer, autumn, and winter.
We will be immersed in one another.
Our Love Feels So Right!
This is a beautiful thing.
As we talk, walk, skip, or run,
We will be thoughtful of everyone.
We will enjoy each other always.
Even as the world gets darker,
Our world will remain illuminated!

Face to face, we linger close to the other.
We feel. We smile. We kiss.
Goodness, that kiss felt so good. That felt so right.
The honey of your heavenly lips still burns
On my lips of clay.
I will try to make you forget your problems
And disappointments.
You, my Princess, are a unique gift from God to me.
Love me tender.
I am so deeply in Love with you.
I want to give you so much.
I need you so incredibly...
And more with each passionate touch.

Congratulations Baby
By Thomas Joe Franks

You and I have a new life together in the making.
My love has found such passionate expression in you.
Do you believe in miracles? I do!
Our souls have now connected.
We both are eagerly awaiting for the next juncture
In our relationship.
We both have expectant views.
I believe they will be of the highest quality
And highly inspirational.
We each desire the other's happiness and welfare.
We have tasted one another's personality.
Lights and sparks have ignited!
We both have strengths that the other needs.
You have brought calmness into my life.
I have brought "playfulness" into yours.
We both feel fully alive.
This excitement for the next 50 years,
We will surely survive.
You have brought me additional common sense.
Hopefully, I have brought you
Additional awareness and motivation...
With a whole lot of love.
You have given me additional wisdom
And youthful thinking!
Our future looks much clearer today
With a good sense of direction for both of us.
Yes, we are independent, yet interdependent as well.
You have given me more patience
In order for me to correct some of my imperfections.
I believe you are a good anchor for me
And I...good wings for you in which to fly.

In the immediate weeks ahead,
Our dreams, plans, aspirations, anticipation, and goals...
Will take on new meaning as we progress
In our relationship of mature love.
Today is a brand new day...
A brand new lease on life...
A creative and eternal miracle of faith, hope, and love!

I'll Never Stop Loving You
By Thomas Joe Franks

I will always love you…
Especially during the long cool summers in Georgia,
Where the breeze is gentle and fresh
Upon your beautiful face.
I will love you in the springtime
When all is green and lovely.
I will love you in the fall…
When the leaves and foliage colors are like a rainbow.
I will love you in the winter,
Especially when the snow is falling
And a fire is in the fireplace.

I will always love you…
Especially when I'm happy or even when I'm sad.
The times, they are a changing,
But not my love for you.
I will love you, especially because you are so gorgeous
And have a pretty face.
I will love you when you get up in the morning
Or when you are hot working in the flower gardens.

I will always love you…
When you are in a good mood or not.
I will love you in the rain
Or when I may be feeling pain.
Our journey together has been filled with respect and love.
I will love you when it's cloudy
Or when the sun shines as bright as noon.
Darling, I will love you until our life on earth is through.

You're Always On My Mind
By Thomas Joe Franks

Throughout the past 18 years of precious time,
You have always been on my mind.
Whether we have been looking at castles on the Rhine
Or viewing the mountains from Neuschwanstein,
You are constantly on my mind
And continue to be my sweet valentine and sunshine.

From the European Alps to the Bavarian Alpines,
You are always on my mind.
Even today as I watch the squirrels and birds
On the old autumn vine,
I'm thinking of you as I hear the clocks chime.
Some men have their Adeline's, Clementine's,
And concubines,
But I have you always on my mind.
Karen, I love you, my sweet kitten feline.

Through the Years
By Thomas Joe Franks

On Friday afternoons like today,
When the air is crisp, cool,
And seems somewhat misty and gray,
Anything is possible, especially when I think
Of our wonderful love.
The leaves will be turning soon my little white dove...
Ahhh... such sweet memories
Of our time together, you and I.
Traveling, dining, shopping, sightseeing,
And your beautiful sigh.
Hopefully, the summer madness is over...
And the autumn freshness covers us like clover.
As you sit down to write in your personal journal,
Never forget the passion and love for you
From this Lieutenant Colonel.
We will grow together through the years,
As we watch the seasons change
After retirement from our careers.
The scenery of colorful foliage and hanging leaves
Will lead us to believe and perceive...
That time is so precious for you and me!
I love you, my Darling Princess, always...
Especially, on cool days like today.
I feel the warmth from your heart.
I know that we will never part.
I love you and miss you incredibly...
And this comes from my tender heart!

When I open My Eyes
Thomas Joe Franks

When I open my eyes in the morning,
You are there.
When I close my eyes in the evening,
You are there.
When I travel down the highway,
You are there.
Wherever I am and wherever I go,
You are on my mind.

Some say that yesterday is gone.
I say they are wrong.
It seems like only yesterday we were on the phone.
And yesterday I knew that I could not be alone.
I had to have you as my very own.
Even though I was bad to the bone,
I was now in a new zone…
The zone of love as solid as a stone in Cupid's throne.

When you and I are far apart,
I feel the void in my tender heart.
I think of you as a beauty of fine art.
I know that you and I will never part.
You are my life, my love, my honey sweet tart.
When you are near, my heart beats off the chart.
I love you Darling…as an incredible piece of art.
My love for you I do impart and my love for you will never part.

Words of Love
By Thomas Joe Franks

Your lips are like sweet ruby red cherries...
When touching mine...they are so fine.
They are warm and have the taste of honey.
Your tender arms around me
Comfort me like toasted sunshine.
Your soft, compassionate, generous, and TRUE VOICE
Let's me know that you are lovely and sweet
And that with you, I made the RIGHT CHOICE.
With you by my side, I will always REJOICE!
My love for you is closer
Now than any time in history.
I recognize you...want you...desire to be near you...
Want to protect you...want to make love to you.
Yearn to comfort you.
Did you know that Lovers live longer?

Karen, You Are The Only One For Me.
By Thomas Joe Franks

If I could spend the next 100 years with you,
It would not be enough.
I just can't seem to get enough of you...
And I don't know why!
I know it's not infatuation.
I know it's not "puppy love".
I know it's not just a mere dream!

I am wide awake.
I love holding you in my arms.
Or just kissing the back of your lovely neck,
Or walking in the park...As long as I'm with you!
I'd be a fool NOT to be in love with you.
If you only realized the depth of my love for you,
You would never let me go in a thousand years.

As I recall the smiles you have painted on my face,
And the sweet memories that go through my mind...
I truly need you all the time.
For you or me...no more tears or pain...
Our love will bring us much heavenly gain.
If I could sing...If I had that type of talent,
I would sing you a thousand love songs and drink Champaign.

One thing I do promise...
I will always impart my love to you...
And truly give you genuine, exciting, passionate romance.
And I will write you a thousand sweet poems of prose...
As you always inspire me with your beautiful glow.
Life with you makes me want to dance and shout,
You have so much passion and influential clout.

My tender little heart beats faster
At just the mention of your name.
I want to hold your body close to mine.
I want to kiss you ever so softly.
I want to look into your emerald green eyes.
When I close my brown eyes,
I still see you looking back at me
To see if I am looking back at you.
I can't remember a happier time than being with you.
Darling, You're The Only One For Me...

The Four Seasons of Loving You (Part 1)
By Thomas Joe Franks

Last winter a year ago in February,
We planted seeds of love.
We tended it with care and affection.
The open air and sunshine made us kids again!
Our soil of patience was sprinkled with much laughter.
Our love began to slowly grow...
And Valentine's Day brought excitement and fun.
Our love life had begun!

Then came Spring and we were on our Pilgrimage of Love.
During our journey, we walked hand in hand...
Sometimes, through fields of happiness,
And sometimes not.
But joy and happiness were always present.
We rediscovered the uncertainties of tomorrow,
But our lives went on...no matter what occurred.
We knew our love was special and we would never part.

Even though at times, we were temporarily apart,
We knew that it was only for a little while.
We knew our destiny.
Last Spring brought us much charm.
The nights were long,
And we had much fun and laughed a lot.
We never got bored.
We listened and learned a lot about each other.

Then Summer appeared
And brought great expectations.
We were alive with hope and excitement.
The coming months got better and better.

Summer brought the best out of us!
We traveled. We played. We loved.
We saw each other in just about every circumstance.
Our lives soared with fruits of love and passion!

As the Fall began to follow the summer,
The countryside was covered
With beautiful, colorful foliage.
Summer was gone, but we were not alone.
We continued our love journey even on the phone.
We did everything to be together.
It was meant to be.
Darling, you know that you are the only one for me.
Our love will never cease.

The Four Seasons Loving You (Part 2)
By Thomas Joe Franks

Soon Winter was nearby...
And coming on strong.
At first, Winter started out on a gentle note.
Hand in hand we walked so many times.
You made my heart ring out with chimes!
During the Winter months, your emerald green eyes
Seemed to say,
"Let's rest by the fireplace and snuggle up with warmth."
Night after night, day after day,
I felt engulfed with the flames of your heart.

Winter did not go away quickly.
It stayed around much longer than expected.
The month of December brought
Many sounds of celebrations.
We loved. We wrote. We made some New Year's resolutions.
The Winter months brought trust, care,
And undying dedication.
February came again. This time we were off to London.
The whole world was busy around us, but we knew
That our best years were ahead of us.
We do enjoy the fruits of our love!

Our seeds of love have been sown.
We are not alone.
Over the past year, we have truly grown.
Now, Spring is here again.
Flowers are everywhere.
We still snuggle up together as often as possible.
Sometimes I dream. You tell me I talk and scream.
Maybe, I eat too much ice cream!

We will never stop loving each another.
We have commitment.
We have something that everybody wants...
And needs!
We have hope.
We have faith. We have love!
Someday people will say,
"We have never seen anyone so in love."

Spring and Love are in the Air
By Thomas Joe Franks

Spring has come.
Love is here.
I had a dream last night…
A lovely dream of you.
As I was walking through a field of dreams,
I heard your gentle voice whispering through the bamboo.
The forest raindrops were falling all around
As we walked between two morning streams.
We make a pretty good team…You and I.

In the dream, I held you close to me in a warm embrace.
We were both happy and filled with joy
As I looked into your beautiful face.
I kissed your hand and smiled
Like a little boy with a new toy.
We stopped and admired all the spring flowers of grace.
We were in such a wonderful place.
This field of dreams it seems
Was filled with incredible love from me to you…
And from you to me as we beamed.

We looked into each other's eyes and knew
That this dream would not end
Because you were more than my friend.
As we walked along the path of the cool crisp morning dew,
I noticed a beautiful twinkle in your eyes.
Your presence gave several clues about you.
You were a woman of statue and ever so wise.
I would make sure that you were never blue…
And always stick beside you like glue.

As the dream ended,
I drew a picture of your face.
This dream of you I wanted to come true.
You will be in my mind and heart
Until there is no time or space.
You are a woman of dignity, value, and virtue.
Your beauty will always leave a lasting trace.
This field of dreams no one can erase.
Spring and love are in the air!

Tremendous Friendship
By Thomas Joe Franks

Her hair is lovely and beautiful as ever.
Her smile is as large as the earth itself.
Like a fresh river, she continues to be a giver.
Our tremendous friendship is truly something to behold,
Because it's been touched by the Refiner's Gold.
Our friendship has stood the test of time,
Even though we had some pain and sorrow.
She is my Sweet Valentine.
Her children call her BLESSED.
She makes them feel special with true success.
She will be my best friend forever without stress.
I can truly say that I have been helped
By a friend who pointed me in the right direction
With holy and praying hands. Her name: Karen Gwyn.

Another Sleepless Night in Washington DC. (Part 1)

By Thomas Joe Franks

Karen, last night, I left my bedroom window open.
I even left a small light on.
I had been talking loudly to someone in my sleep.
The rain was coming down gently.
I dreamed you were lying beside me.
Suddenly, I was awakened from my dreams.
I looked into your incredible face.
The silhouette of your sweet body intrigued me.
I could hear the rain outside.
I held you in my arms. I pulled you close to my chest.
We talked. We laughed. We kissed.
You said, "Thomas Joe, I will never let you go."
I responded, "Wonderful...Gung Ho...Geronimo!"
We danced. We whispered. We sighed.
We held each other ever so closely.
The full moon was bright.
I want you to know that
You should always be beside me.
That is where I want you to be...
So tenderly!
I long to see and feel your beautiful face...
I feel your heart beating.
I feel your body breathing
As you lie beside me in our bed.
I close my eyes.
No matter what I do,
I can't get enough of you.
What am I to do?
As we lay side by side, I heard the cars go by below...
I even heard one of my favorite songs

On one of the car radios.
I long to be with you. I really want to hold you...
To hear you talk, laugh, and play.
Dance with me...Dance to the music.
How I do need you...Somehow, I will make it thru the day.
Oh yes, we have had a lot of phone conversations.
Your voice, I know quite well…
I know your laugh... your sigh.
I know your smile. How could I be so lonely?
How could I miss you so much?
In my heart, I carry you with me.
You are now a big part of me...A beautiful part…
I never want to be without you…So here I am...
Lying here thinking about you...
While it is still raining outside.
I look up at the ceiling. I close my eyes. I listen.
I open my eyes again. I look for you. You are gone.
The dream is over. Here I am...alone again.
Another Sleepless Night in Washington DC.

Another Sleepless Night in Washington DC. (Part 2)

By Thomas Joe Franks

You were holding me in your arms with your charm.
You were pulling me close to you.
We talked about dancing.
We heard our own song through the rain.
We kissed. We held one another.
We again vowed that we would never let the other go.
Finally, the dream vanished...and I was alone again.
I knew then that it would be another
Sleepless Night in Washington.
I can still smell your sweet perfume.
And feel your silky blonde hair upon my shoulder.
I can feel you holding me close to you.
We will dance again...beneath the pale moonlight.
The rain is still coming down.
Together, we are so hot.
Every day I see you...in my thoughts and mind.
I long to be with you, my Darling Princess!
I always want to be able to reach over
And tenderly run my fingers through your soft silky hair.
I long to kiss your sweet lips again...
To feel your beautiful face...your neck...your arms around me.
I love to feel your breath upon my neck...
I reminisced again...Another Sleepless Night in D.C.
As I continued to dream,
You lay there ever so gently sound sleep.
I close my eyes expecting to wake up with you
In my arms...
No matter what I do anymore, I envision you doing it with me.
We will soon be with one another again.
As I am driving, I hear one of our favorite songs...

And I imagine you in the seat next beside me...
Sharing the music...and smiling all the while.
I long to be with you and take you home with me...
To hold your hand again in the movie theater.
I want to hear you laugh again...
See you dance with me again...
As your body sways from side to side with the music.
Our souls touch one another.
I need you so much, I really do!
I don't know how I made it through before without you,
Do You?
We have so many phone conversations behind us.
I know your voice so well...
As I said before, I know your laugh...
Your lips... your pretty face.
I even know how your voice sounds when you smile.

Another Sleepless Night in Washington DC. (Part 3)
By Thomas Joe Franks

Sometimes, I have even heard a teardrop in your voice.
That is when, I want to reach across the ocean
And kiss away your anxiety, cares, and fears.
I want to take away all your heartache...
Your loneliness, your tears.
Every day, I carry you with me in my tender heart.
You have become a part of me...
And now, I never want to be without you.
So now I lie here...listening to the falling rain...
For a brief moment, I see us together in my mind.
I close my eyes...searching for your beautiful smile...
I listen for your voice...
And then I hear you say,
"Goodnight my sweet love... I love you!"
I opened my eyes and you were gone.
And now, I am still alone...I am here...You are there...
Another Sleepless Night in Washington D.C...without you!

Happy Valentine's Day 2008
(To Karen My Love)
By Thomas Joe Franks

One more time I want to say,
"You mean the world to me every day."
All the little things you convey…
Sweet words and beautiful smiles you display…
More lovely than a thousand bouquets.
I will continue to love you…come what may.
Being with you is such a wonderful, sweet life array.
You have made my life complete today as always!

Valentine, you are my true love and friend…
Even more than my Black Beauty Benz.
My feelings for you will never end.
Beyond my heart and soul, your love transcends.
My loving arms for you, my Love, always extend.
Our love for one another does not depend
Upon circumstances or situations that may offend.
Our love is wrapped up in joy that continues to ascend.

Your warmth is like the morning sunrise.
Your hidden talents sometimes take me by surprise.
You have melted my cold, cold heart inside…
And taken away my lonely disguise.
Your emerald green eyes are such a delightful prize.
New horizons await us as we explore the ocean blue skies.
Your sweetness and calmness continue to make me wise.
You are the most incredible Valentine to ever live,
I must reply.

The Prince and Princess Together
By Thomas Joe Franks

A short time ago,
A romantic Prince met his beautiful Princess under a
Florida rainbow.
At first, the young Prince was stunned
By her brilliant glow,
But he managed to say a sweet "Hello"!
As the conversation began to flow,
The Prince knew in his tender heart
That he had been shot with the cupid's bow!

The days of summer 2002 were such a blast,
As the courageous Prince
Spent time with this incredible lass.
Soon the days ended ever so fast,
For a short while, the Prince and Princess
Parted company greatly aghast.
The Prince longed for this
Fabulous goddess-like creation of class.
He just knew that soon, he would see her again at last!

Together again,
We did begin.
We have been so busy enjoying our love within.
Together again,
We have played to win.
We have pledged to live together through "thick and thin".

As we sit together and relive the good times,
Our tender hearts will forever chime.
Our lives will mellow with grace through Father time.

We have lost some of our innocence
Along the journey climb.
We now share the secrets of our hearts one at a time.
We know that summers are not an endless lifetime!

Autumn 2005 at Lorton, VA (To: Karen)
By Thomas Joe Franks

Let me tell you about this wonderful woman I know.
She wears a smile everywhere she goes!
Let me tell you what she means to me.
She is like a breath of fresh air in the autumn wind!
When I am NOT with her, it's difficult to breathe.
I know that there must be something more to this.
I think I know what it is...
She is the love that I have been searching for!

The day has come when I finally see...
That from now until forever...She is the one for me!
I don't want to go back to the "good old days".
Those were the BKF (Before Karen Franks) days...
Before her heart was mine.
I don't want to go back to those lonely BFK days.
Now every day is a good day because she
Makes my day a very happy and fulfilling day!

She smiles a lot with her beautiful face.
Almost daily, I see a glow in her eyes.
I see what we are together...incredibly in love.
When I shut my eyes at night,
I see us holding each other tight and kissing
In the moon light!
Do you really know how she makes me feel?
She makes me feel as if all my important dreams
Have been fulfilled!

When she came into my life,
All the clouds cleared...and the sun began to shine!
Now time stands still because our love is so real!

Chances are most people see that our love will never part.
Chances are most know that she is
The only one for my heart.
I never knew what it was like to be loved this much.
Our future holds so much joy...
I am so grateful to be with you.
My life would not be complete with anyone but you!

Falling In Love With You
By Thomas Joe Franks

Once upon a time in Lakeland with you,
I stood beside you overlooking the lake so blue.
I looked down and saw our reflection of two...
On the clear water with such a panoramic view.
At that moment, I knew it would be only you!
I was so captivated by your beauty so true.

I closed my eyes, but you remained in my mind like glue.
My heart was swept away like a run-away canoe!
Your love has captivated me like two bears in a zoo.
Now my journey of love is way past due...
I feel like a big caribou or perhaps a kangaroo
That have met for the first time
At a wonderful point of rendezvous.

The sun and moon now glisten and remind me
Of the beauty of Oahu.
Your incredible beauty reflects your love
Through and through,
Because you have captured my tender little heart
Like Winnie the Pooh!
Your beauty has set my blazing heart
On fire like a hot barbecue!
"I'm raging out of control", says who?
Is it because I have been quenched
By your kisses and tenderness too?

Your lips hold me captivated like exquisite bars of bamboo.
Your embrace takes my breath away
As we travel on Love Avenue!
Sleep is so sweet now as I dream of you.

My thoughts of you are pure, warm,
And like the morning dew.
With you, I will never be alone, even in Timbuktu.
Your dreams are my dreams...Oh, how I love you!

Every time I see you...every time I hold you,
Every time I kiss you...Every time I whisper to you,
My heart races like the horses in Peru.
You have turned me into a wild stallion
With golden horseshoes.
My love for you is way past due! What am I to do?
I'm falling in love with Karen...so fresh and anew.

Happy 56th Birthday to the Queen of Lakeland (6 Feb 2004)
By Thomas Joe Franks

Karen Gwyn, you have now become
My beautiful wife and friend.
Do you really know how much you are worth?
You are worth more than all the earth!

Your parents knew that you were a beautiful baby.
They knew that you would grow.
They knew that you would become strong.
You have known great joy.
You have known great pain.
For tears, God has given you sunshine.
For night, He has given you day.
For the desert, He has given you rain.

When you look in the mirror, what do you see?
You see a beautiful woman,
A person of value and great gain.
Over the years you have learned
To appreciate this time of year...
Another birthday... another year!
What are you about?
You are about kindness, sharing,
Helping others, and caring.
You are wonderful person...
A sweet person... beautiful woman.
And no one can take that away from you!

The older you get, the more graceful you become.
With age comes beauty and style.
You represent loveliness in every way.

The warmth of your tender touch
And your sweet love have given me so much.
Your sweetness is like a water spring flowing over a stone.
I know I will never again be alone.
I touch your beautiful face.
I then kiss your ruby red lips.
I begin to feel my heartbeat racing. I then slowly lead you to my bed!

The warmth of your breast I feel upon my hairy chest.
You turn your face to look into my eyes.
I know that I love you more
Each time we make love.
I have no doubts that we will enjoy one another
For another 50 years!
I love you, Tommy Joe

Happy Birthday Karen (Feb 6, 2005)
By Thomas Joe Franks

We have been together now for three years,
Yet it seems like yesterday we met.
You have opened my heart to new heights without fears.
You are more than just my friend.
You are my sweet, sweet Karen and beautiful wife!
You have put a brand new heart within me that transcends.

You make me feel so happy and strong.
No word can describe the joy you bring to me!
I am so glad that we found each other...We belong!
We chose each other and fell in love.
I am so fortunate to have you as my incredible wife!
You may be from earth, but God sent you to me from
Planet Heaven.

To me you are the perfect woman.
You make me feel complete.
You make me feel like a real he-man and hero.
The little things you do for me are so important and good.
Mere words could never convey...
The tenderness you bring to me
Which is never misunderstood!

Your sweet smile...your playful glance,
Your warm caress...Your honey bee kisses...
You mean more to me than a hundred years of romance!
I will treasure you always, my Love!
Happy Birthday, my sweet Karen.
I love you more today than yesterday, my heavenly Dove.

Your sweet love and support we share.
The world stands still when I am with you!
Happy Birthday My Beautiful Queen beyond compare!
Darling, it's your birthday…
I wouldn't change a thing about you.
I love you just the way you are, my gorgeous Bouquet!

Easter 2007 With Karen
By Thomas Joe Franks

The cold dark clouds of winter are behind us.
The fresh smell of spring flowers
And gentle breezes are before us.
The glittering sunshine brings forth hope...
The resurrection hope.
As we celebrate the resurrection of Jesus Christ,
We also celebrate life with each other,
Especially new beginnings that are all around us.

Easter with Karen awakens so many emotions within me.
I reflect on the first Easter that we knew each other.
You are such a beautiful bright star
That has brought me hope.
You are so warm and tender with so much charm.
I couldn't help myself.
I fell in love with you!

This Easter as we rejoice and celebrate
This special event together,
I will not forget that God created you
For me and once again...
Gave me faith, hope, and love!
As I look into your emerald green eyes,
I thank Him every day for the sunshine
That you bring to me.
The Easter lilies, bunny rabbits, Easter eggs,
Fresh flowers, palm trees...
Remind me that every day is Easter with you. I love you!

Easter With Karen
By Thomas Joe Franks

This time of year is a good time to love you;
Easter always refreshes us and gives us life anew.
Easter brings us love and reminds us
Of a Man and a Cross.
He died for us a long time ago
So that we would not suffer loss.
He arose three days later.
They could not keep Him in the ground
Because He is the Creator.

I am so glad that we are together
To celebrate another Easter...regardless of the weather!
Christ loves us so much as you know.
He paid the ultimate price for a debt He did not owe.
We are together because of what He did a long time ago.
The nails pierced his hands
So that we could hold hands in the snow.

A crown of thorns was placed upon his head.
They put many stripes upon His back as He bled.
He died on that cross renowned.
They buried Him, but they could not
Keep Him in the ground.
Jesus was resurrected after He had conquered
Death and hell;
Thus our redemption was given to us to forever tell.

Easter is a special time of year to love you.
You are such a most wonderful treasure
For me to daily view.
You are so easy to love.

You came into my life when my heart
Needed mending from above.
I was confused and you opened your arms wide to help me.
You stood by me and comforted me...
Everything would be alright, you decreed.

You are now my Easter Angel.
You have shown me incredible love from Heaven!
I need you, it's true.
Your love is stronger now than when we met in 2002.
You have restored my hope, faith, love, and confidence
Even without a toupee.
Thank you for another wonderful Easter Day!

My Darling Karen (Easter 2008)
By Thomas Joe Franks

Winter has come and gone. Spring is before us.
The smell of fresh flowers, gentle breezes,
And glittering sunshine
Are so revitalizing...Spring is in the air.
Spring represents the resurrection of hope.
We celebrate the resurrection of Jesus Christ as significant.
It brings a new beginning for all of us.
Jesus died on the Cross...He now lives.
We reflect on His promises.
We give thanks to Him... the One
Who holds the stars in His Hands.

He moves the waves of the seas.
We rejoice in the Love that He has created in us.
We glance at the sky each day
And thank Him for the sunshine.
He has given us life all together.
We see His hand in the events all around us.
We know that His love grows
In our gentle breeze of acceptance.
He lifts us up today.
We feel His love.
We feel His forgiveness.

We feel His understanding...We feel His encouragement.
He helps us to find our way.
Today, we sing a new song.
We sing a song of praise to our King.
Music soothes our soul.
We thank You Lord for Your goodness.
We thank You Lord for your grace and love.

You died on that old rugged cross.
You have given us a brand new start.

Karen, if I could show the world all your beauty,
I would paint it on canvass for all to see.
My Easter wish is that you will always be with me
On this special day!
We have love... We have sweet joy...
We have beauty in our living.
Our love is more wonderful each day.
Our hopes, dreams, and times of joy
Have exceeded my expectations.
Our love brings us closer together each day.
With each passing day, I love you more and more,
My Darling.
With this Easter cross and heart,
I give you my love on
This Easter Day (2008)!

I Always Want You To Feel Loved
By Thomas Joe Franks

Feeling loved is a beautiful thing! It's incredible! I always want you to feel loved by me. Most people will do just about anything to have this lovely feeling. It is so fulfilling and rewarding. I will always give you my love freely. Loving you makes me feel loved as well. When I look into your eyes…without saying a word…I want to make you feel like you are the most important and incredible woman in the world.

I want you to know that you are special to me! I can't seem to get enough of you…My eyes will always speak to you. Your eyes sparkle even in the night. I want to always make you feel loved…and special. I care about you so much. I promise, I will never be embarrassed to kiss you or hold you close to me in public. I will always hold your hand and kiss it ever so sensually. That's the way I am.

Karen, Darling, I want you to feel loved when you wake up each morning and when you go to bed at night. I will hold you and stroke your beautiful blonde hair. I will kiss your ruby red lips and even massage your little feet. My eyes will continue to tell you how beautiful you are throughout the day. I will try to remember the little things that make you happy.

Sometimes, I will call you on the telephone…without any good reason…other than to say, "I love you". Sometimes, I may do something small or something simple for you…just because I love you. For example, it may be a kiss or a touch or a small little card…But I will continue to show you that I am constantly thinking about you and want you to know this.

I also want you to know that through all things, you are the love of my life and I will be true and faithful to you. At times, I will be compassionate and passionate as well. You will know that I am more than just your best friend. You will feel appreciated! You will feel loved. You will always feel "like a beautiful woman"! My tender brown eyes and compassionate heart will display sweetness and innocence in your world all around you. Sometimes, we may not always agree, but I will acknowledge your opinion and your feelings and respect them as such. You will feel loved by me. When you walk into a room where I am standing or sitting, I will not be able to keep my eyes off you. In a good sense, I will watch your every move...and you do have a lot of good moves! Oh, yeah! That's when you will know and feel as if...We are the only two people in the room! Hello!

I will be honest and genuine about my feelings. I will always make you smile.
You will feel loved because you will see the smile on my face as I look at you.
You will hear my tender whispers in your ears. You will know that you make my heart jump louder and faster. You will also know that you can be open with me on any issue. When you touch me, I will become jelly in your arms. Through the years, the twinkle in my eyes will get even brighter! I love you...Tommy.

I Love You for Being You!
By Thomas Joe Franks

When I first saw you with your beautiful smile and perfect emerald green eyes,
I felt as if we were always meant to be with each other. Your sweet soul reflected kindness and compassion for others, especially me. Sometimes, my heart would almost stop beating. Of course, we had a second meeting.

I stopped eating for days because meeting you for the first time was so unforgettable. The beauty of your face was so incredible. You were always on my mind. You softened up my heart to be more kind and refined. Watching your sexy body was like watching two stars collide generating a million sparks in the Galaxy. The fire was burning and my mind was just seconds away from exploding.

Soon, I realized that without you...I couldn't breathe, I couldn't think, I couldn't see straight, I couldn't eat. I knew that I wanted you to be mine. When describing your beauty and my love for you, words became so small. Sometimes, I find myself hitting a blank wall searching for the right words to tell our love story.

When I am in your presence, you smell like a bed of endless rose pedals...red, yellow, pink, purple, orange, and burgundy. Surely the earth never had such an aromatic fragrance before. These are just a few things that I remember about our first weeks, months, and years together on Planet Earth. I love you, Tommy (Aug 2007)

I See a Beautiful Woman!
Written to Karen...22 July 2002
By Thomas Joe Franks

I see a beautiful woman...who loves me.
She is blossoming forth as a red, red rose!
She reminds me of the early rain in Spain.
Her love and care for me make me feel
As free as a giant oak tree in the rain.
Our special love experiences grow
Every day to a higher plane.

I see a beautiful woman...who needs me!
She is opening up as a beautiful and colorful butterfly.
Setting herself free...free from despair and despondency...
Free from the past...
Free from all guilt and blame.

I see a beautiful woman discovering her beauty,
The beauty inside her heart and soul.
I also see the beauty that surrounds her special moves...
With each new day bringing such bright rays of sunshine,
Especially into the lives of others and mine.

I see a beautiful woman...who wants me!
She has a vision for her life and mine.
The clouds have vanished
And the fog has lifted.
The future looks bright ahead.

I see a beautiful woman...who cares for me!
She is letting go of any excess baggage,
And letting go of any past wrongs or pain.
Her worth, happiness, and joy have now
Become a tremendous gain without chains.

I see a beautiful woman...who longs for me!
She is finding out who she really is.
She is finding freedom in discovering true love...
And also knowing how to love herself...
As I love her.

I see a beautiful woman...
With whom I want to live the rest of my life!
She is evolving beyond
Her wildest dreams and expectations.
She is filled with passion, excitement, and enthusiasm.
Inside her heart and soul, she will never grow old...
And the Beauty of it is...
She loves me incredibly more
Than all the gold and words ever told.

Incredible Karen (Mother's Day 2007)
By Thomas Joe Franks

A mother's love determines how
We love ourselves and others.
A mother's love determines how
Much we like certain foods.
Karen is such a mother.

Without a mother's love our universe would be
Filled with sadness and pain,
But we are born into a world with a mother
Who greets our first cries with joy.
Karen is such a mother.

Mothers seem to kiss the hurts away.
A mother's touch makes us get well so fast.
As long as Mothers are around,
We know that we have the greatest gift of all…Love.
Karen is such an incredible mother.

As a mother, Karen has graced us with her smile.
She has forgiven us for our mistakes.
Karen has given us hope and passion anew.
Her unmovable faith in us has made us strong.
Karen is such a mother.

A mother's love…loves us as we learn to love.
A mother's heart turns our hearts toward home.
A mother's heart turns our hearts toward God.
We have become all that we are today because of our
Mother's love.
Karen is such a mother…Incredible "Mother"!

Until I met Karen, I thought I knew
A thing or two about beauty.
Since I met Karen, I have found out what love is all about.
She has turned my sadness to joy...
And turned my happiness into more abundant living.
Karen is an incredible mother
And virtuous and honorable wife.
I love you... Tommy

Your Love Makes My Day (Summer 2007)
By Thomas Joe Franks

Your love is like a bright hurricane lantern.
Your love is sexy and lights my way every day.
You uplift my spirits and state of mind,
When skies are gray and I feel confined.
Your love is like a rushing wave of hope.
You lift me higher and higher
Like a mountain's slope.
Your tender love I incredibly admire.
You set my steamy body aflame like a wild brush fire!
You take away my breath with deep sensual desire.

My love for you will never die.
My love for you is always and forever I cannot deny.
Your love is more than a beautiful red, red rose.
Your love touches my manly soul.
When I think of your beauty to behold,
It reminds me of pure, expensive gold.
Your eyes are so bright and emerald green,
You are indeed my sunshine queen.
I just wanted to write this poem to remind you
That "I love you" and always will, it's true!

Upon My Return To Your Loving Arms
By Thomas Joe Franks

The first thing I will do is hold you close to me…
So I can feel your hot body next to mine!
I'm sure our pulse will be beating faster than a flaming bee.
I will hold you ever so tightly
As your green eyes beam brightly.
Yes, I desperately love you
Like no other on the face of this earth.
I feel like I have been re-birthed.

The day moves from sunrise to sunset.
As I hold you in my arms,
You seduce me with your charm!
In my heart, our moments will last forever!
You are so gifted and so clever. As I hold you in my arms,
I smell your blonde hair as the wind blows it across my face.

Next, I gently take my hands
And bring your face close to mine.
Your slender neck looks so divine. Our arms are intertwined.
You are wrapped around me so fine.
We both hear music in the background.
Love songs heighten our emotions sublime.
During this lovely moment, our passion is primed.

As I hold you in my loving arms,
The next thing I will do is…kiss your ruby red lips!
My kiss is full of fire and tenderness…
Which certainly lets you know
How much I care…How much I missed you.
I will always kiss you with passion and desire.
Why? Because I long for you like cold yeans for fire!

I suddenly hear your joyous laughter.
I know that everything is all right.
You caress my gentle soul and spirit.
Our lives together fill with such richness…
It is so wonderful to be with you during our prime time.
We are so blessed to be free and productive
As an orange blossom tree! Kiss me now. Kiss me quick.
Kiss me sweet with your honey dew lips.

Finally, as I hold you close to me. I will love you indefinitely.
We will love like two inseparable Australian turtledoves…
As we laugh and talk and make love thereof.
I will always love you…
Even as I lose more of my hair.
Over the years, our bodies may get slower,
However, I promise not to abuse your hair blower.
I am not an animal in a cave,
But I will always be your love slave!

A Letter To My Darling Princess
By Thomas Joe Franks

When you wake up in the early morning hours, think of me. I know winter is coming, but spring and summer will follow. It won't be long. Think of me. Even now… this moment, I'm there with you in spirit and thought! Tonight, as you look at the beautiful moon overhead, think of me. I'll be under the same sky looking at the same moon! I will take a deep breath and sigh…just dreaming of the time we'll be together again.
It won't be long, my Love.

As the days are short and the nights are long and cold, think of me. I'll be there with you to keep you warm in your thoughts and feelings. I don't like wintry times because they are so chilly, nippy, bleak, and cold. And I have a tender, warm, teddy bear heart. Golden brown sand beneath my feet is much better than frost and ice beneath my feet. Therefore, as you leisurely stroll down the beach, think of me because I will be thinking of you. As the colorful autumn leaves begin to fall from the hard wood trees and the air is crisp, think of me. As you smell the wood burning from the neighborhood fireplaces with the live smells of winter, I'll be there with you…in heart, soul, and spirit. I believe in you. I believe that you are someone so special…so inspiring…so fabulous…so incredible and so amazing. You have so much to offer to our society and communities. As you dream and ponder about our future, think of me!

Soon, the cold winter winds will begin to blow. Snow will come. Icicles will hang from various roof tops and magnanimous buildings. The snow ploughs will be out in the early morning snow. During the winter weather as you sit by a warm fire, think of me. I'll be there to share your thoughts with you, to hold you, to love you, and rub your tense back and neck in front of the crackling fireplace. Think of me because I'll be thinking of you. Never forget. Summer is coming soon. It always comes after the spring and winter. At that time, you will no longer have to hold back your tears of joy. You will no longer have to pretend that all is right with the world. I'll be with you...and the world will be right because we will be together for another 50 winters, but this time, they will be wonderful...Because we will be in Winter Wonderland. We will remember the good times...and experience a whole new world! Baby, summer is coming!

PART 2

A Letter To Mama
When I Was 35 Years Old
By Thomas Joe Franks

Dear Mama,

I wish that we would have had more time to spend together while you were here. But with all of us children (seven in all), you had to work a lot to keep food on the table and shoes on our little feet. There were a lot of things that I should have said while you were here, but I didn't...so, I'll say them now.

Mama, I want to say "Thank-you" for nursing me back to health and praying for me when both of my small arms and hands were burned to a dull black...the time I fell into the open fireplace. You called on your God to help me and He heard you. And remember the time that you prayed for me while I was still in your womb. You asked for God's protection over me. Then, when I was eight years old, you stayed up all night with me, prayed, and cared for me because I had appendicitis. You prayed to your God. He intervened. Now, many years later, I am still well. Thank you.

Mama, I can remember you getting upset with us at times, but we always knew you loved us. I now have four children of my own. I do understand. Mama, I love you and I want you to forgive me for causing you pain and heartaches at times. Another time you saved my life. I was driving too fast. You told me to slow down. I reluctantly did. Immediately afterwards, the right front tire exploded. Your request and warning saved our lives that day. Mama, thanks...I was too young to die!

The tears, sweat, blood, and agony that was given for us children (seven) was a great sacrifice on your part. I remember in 1953 while you were giving birth to our little sister, you almost died, but somehow God let you live a few more years on this planet. Yes, you shed many a tear drop for us, especially me. And I'll always be grateful to you for giving me life and sound moral principles. Mama, there were times that I was away from home a long time. You prayed for me. You bragged on me. Even when I was wrong, you encouraged me.

"Mama, I want to say one more thing...I miss you with all my heart.
I look forward to seeing you again. Mama, tomorrow, I'll be 35 years old.
What's that Mama? Yes, I do have tears in my eyes...and it feels good to
cry because these tears are not tears of sorrow, but joy...the joy of having
you for a mother." With all my love, Your son...
Thomas Joe

NOTE: My mother died in 1969, but I wrote her this letter on 28 Sep 1981. Yes, I know that we cannot communicate with our loved ones in heaven; however, for my own health and welfare, I wanted to write down some things that perhaps had never been said before... or had gone unsaid while Mom was still living. And, no, I did not mail the letter either because I did not know how much postage it would take to mail it to Planet Heaven!

Mother

By Thomas Joe Franks

Mother, you are so SPECIAL.
You gave me warmth when I was cold.
I was afraid, but you were bold.
My strength had gone,
But YOU were strong.
I had a fever on my brow,
You came and spoke and prayed aloud.
A beautiful smile came over your face
When you saw the Lord's amazing grace.

Mother, you are SPECIAL.
Your children rise up and call you blessed.
Now, after many years you can get some rest.
Your fervent prayers have stood the test
Because YOU were not afraid to invest.
Concerning me as your son, abortion never entered your mind.
You were a woman so very kind.
Mama, you stood the test of time and won.
Your life in Heaven has begun!

In Memory of: Mrs. Eva (Bearden) Franks

Continue to March, Anointed Woman of God

This poem is for all the women of God.
By Thomas Joe Franks

Continue to arise, O woman of God.
See what God has given you.
God has laid many things upon your heart.
Rise up, go forth, and continue to restore.

God has given you treasures within.
His anointing, He has placed upon you.
Many will be coming for their oil of joy…
So, expand your wings and fly higher still.

Continue to arise in your God-given gifts,
For this is your finest hour.
Go forth in the Lord's holy might,
Empowered and ignited with a Godly flame of fire.

God has given you an incredible calling
To go forth and impact your world for Him.
Don't hold back or limit yourself,
Let His power arise within you.

You have a special message to give
To those who have lost their way.
You are truly making a difference
As you hear His voice and obey.

You shall be strengthened in the Name of the Lord
As you begin to arise to new heights of Joy.
The Holy Spirit will assist you in conquering doubts
Because you know your God-given rights with Godly clout.

You will continue to be transformed
As you renew and expand the vision He has given you.
Continue to arise, O woman of excellence and truth...
Because God is bringing you into an anointed break-through.

Who is this Man?
(Written from Heidelberg Germany)
By Thomas Joe Franks

I was once dead,
But NOW I have been re-created.
I was on my way to hell,
But NOW I am on the road to Glory.
I was lost, lonely, and cold,
But NOW He has found me.
I was in total bondage,
But NOW He has set me FREE.
I was born into sin a loser,
But NOW I am a born again Winner.
I was so empty and hopeless without power,
But NOW I am filled with His faith and energy.
I felt so alone without joy,
But NOW He has given me the Holy Comforter.
I was in shambles,
But NOW I have a brand new Landlord.
I felt so unloved,
But NOW I have a great Lover.
Who is this Man?
Who is this Landlord?
Who is this Lover?
This Man is Jesus, the Lover of my soul.

Who Are The Pohick Dixie Dolls?
Lorton, VA
By Thomas Joe Franks

The Pohick Dixie Dolls shine as brilliant stars
In the moonlight skies.
They are the "Apple" of God's eyes. When you see them,
Their faces beam with radiant smiles.
When they walk into a room, you can feel
Their warmth, love, and style,
And smell their aromatic and
Sweet fragrant perfume from above.
As the raindrops fall from time to time,
The Dixie Dolls continue to shine in their prime.
The Dixie Dolls are like the petals of an orchid flower…
Their love continues to bud, blossom,
And mature with power.
Each life they touch becomes even taller like a strong tower.

If you have been touched and blessed
By the presence of the Dixie Dolls,
Your days will certainly not be filled with doom and gloom.
They will put a smile on your face. You will laugh…
You will talk…
You will find kindness and grace.
Each Dixie Doll is incredibly talented
In her own field of space.
Sometimes, they are as carefree as a child.
Other times, they act a little untamed and wild… but yet
mild.
The Dixie Dolls are beautiful, strikingly stunning,
And easy on the eyes.
These women are virtuous and more priceless
Than rubies and diamonds.

The Dolls are the top drawer prize, their husbands
And friends cannot deny!

Their good deeds and fruit of their hands...
Will be praised in the gates
Throughout the land. Strength, honor, and wisdom
Are in their hearts.
Words from their sweet lips
Make an impact like the fine arts.
Over the years, they have matured like burgundy wine.
Each day, these Pohick Dixie Dolls
Become more beautiful and refined.
More elegant ladies, you will never meet on this earth
Than these four ladies of extraordinary and incredible
worth.
Their words are like an orchestra
Playing sweet music to your heart.
As you converse with each one,
You will be dazzled right from the start.

Destiny and time are awe-inspiring and sublime.
Sweet dreams of yesterday are filled
With inspirations of every kind.
Life should be filled with passion
That reinvigorates your mind.
Thoughts of Heaven should never be far away,
Especially when the Dixie Dolls make you feel special
As a rose in a bouquet.
The beauty of the Dolls is so uncommonly rare...
That one cannot truly fathom or compare!
Once in every lifetime, someone comes along
Who truly makes you feel like you belong.
These special angels...The Pohick Dixie Dolls...
God has truly sent along. He cannot be wrong!

Falling in Love
By Thomas Joe Franks

Passion rules when a man and woman fall in love.
The angels in Heaven are all looking on
Like mourning doves.
Sometimes, you feel like you are walking on air...
Your heart is beating beyond compare.
You have been swept off your feet.
You have given your love complete.
Your two hearts have become one.
Your life together has begun.
The future looks bright ahead.
You both are about to be wed.
What will the future bring?
Certainly a couple of beautiful wedding rings.
Promises will be made...
And your commitments will be weighed.
Sweet and pure will be your wedding day!
Your love for each other will be forever and always.
May the blessings from Heaven continue to reign upon you.
May your love for each other be stronger than glue.
This wedding is no accident one can truly see.
You both look happy together, we all agree.
Angels will be near you from the very start.
As a couple in love, may you prosper
And never grow apart.
Remember, loving one another on this earth...
Is time well spent.
Heaven has brought you together for this special event!

Today!
By Thomas Joe Franks

Today is another payday.
We are still here, it is quite clear.
Our future is as bright as the sun at noonday.
Our Maker is never too far away...to say,
"Child, I have kept you and protected you
Even before your first birthday.
Planet Earth is where you live today.
But in eternity, you will live with Me always.
My work in you is NOT finished yet.
But don't worry My child. Don't fret.
Your life with Me, you will never regret."

We live moment by moment...day by day.
Yet, all we really have is today!
Sure, we are made of clay.
And sometimes, in disarray.
Even in the best of times, the clouds may become gray.
But we continue to pray.
There is no other way.
Just let me say... "There will come a day
When the world will see no more delay or dismay.
Everything will be okay."

All we really have is today!
One day soon, we will eat at Heaven's buffet...
While the devil and his strays
Will have hell to pay...
Without delay!
It will be their doomsday.
Hey, hey, hey...
We will be happy and gay

Because we obeyed.
Even now, we can smell the aroma of Heaven's bouquets.

In Heaven, we will dine in beautiful cafes,
Never under a cloud of doubt or dismay!
Our coronation and celebration will convey
And take away...
All our concerns of yesterday.
The Son will portray
All Goodness, all Mercy, all Grace, and be our Mainstay.
Every day will be a holyday.
In Heaven, we will forever stay.
But right now, all we really have is today!

I Feel Your Pain
By Thomas Joe Franks

Sometimes when we are betrayed or treated badly,
The pain can be overwhelming and crushing.
Sometimes, it's deliberate...
And sometimes it's just ignorance.
It really hurts when it's someone close to us
Or a fellow Christian.
Sometimes, the pain lingers and stays for a while
And the tears begin to flow, but through it all,
We are NOT alone.
You did not fail. You did nothing wrong.

Your pain is His pain.
Turn it over to Him.
He truly understands,
Especially since you were only trying to help.
Someone said, "Every good deed never goes unpunished."
Your kind and generous heart was betrayed.
But the rising Son has overshadowed you with His LOVE.
Instead of more pain, He is replacing it with JOY.

Sometimes our pain is self-inflicted and self-chosen.
But not so in many cases.
You were working for God in what you were doing
And God was well pleased in what He saw.
This was a trick of the enemy to detour you
From your tranquility.
The tender Hands of God...the Great Potter
Is once again fashioning your heart of clay
With the moisture of His own sacred tears.

A View from My Window...Friends
By Thomas Joe Franks

As I stood looking out my bedroom window,
Contemplating my life,
I saw a mighty tall oak tree not far from my windowpane.
It stood majestic by the side of the building...
Its branches reaching out in all directions...
Fresh rain resting upon them. The rain continued to fall...
And the branches continued to stretch outward.
They drooped a little from the heaviness of the water,
But the tree remained standing firm.
That's when I thought of my friends with great faith.

Sometimes, the world and circumstances
Can unexpectedly burden us with
All kinds of unforeseen things,
Yet like this mighty tall oak tree,
We persevere! Life may appear bleak,
But the tall tree stands proud...
Even when stripped of its beautiful green leaves
And life force.
It finds the good in the barren ground...
Knowing that nutrients will come and rejuvenate its life.
When times appear the bleakest, good somehow prevails.
That's when I think of my friends with great faith...
God will not let you fail.

We all appreciate what we have in the present.
Sometimes, we wonder if the storm will ever end.
Then spring comes and the warm sunlight returns.
Things become green again...
And the mighty tree begins to bud with new life.
We awaken to sunny days

And the world now looks so different!
Storms come and go. Clouds disperse.
The oak tree stands!

Some of our friends are like this mighty tall oak tree.
You have withstood so many pitfalls.
You are a delight to be around.
Fear has no hold on you. You always keep going.
You find solace.
In God's green Earth…And the people of this Earth.
You live each day as it comes…
You face adversities knowing that
At some point the sun will shine again!
Oh yeah, the wind blows,
The rain falls, but you and the oak tree stand firm!
You both have an inner strength to get you
Through the day and the storm.

In our day and age, we look for heroes.
I have found some, yet, they do not fight as Military
soldiers in an Army.
No, but they do live life to its fullest…
Continuing when others have quit. They give joy to others.
Their inner strength radiates from them to others.
This is great gift.
I appreciate friends who help others. Thank you.
Just knowing you as friends has made me
One of the richest people in the world.
Like the tall oak tree outside my window,
you will continue to stand tall,
Proud, and refreshed. Thanks for being my friends.
You know who you are!

To Our True Friends
By: Thomas Joe Franks

In this day and age, true friends are hard to find,
But you have a wonderful way in which
You came into our lives.
Your words are always on time.
We are so happy you are friends forever
And not just part time.

It seems we have been together for many years.
We have shared so many mysteries of our lives
Together without fear.
Laughter, tears, and joy have been seen in our eyes,
And true friendship we have found in you
As a tremendous prize.

We are not saying goodbye,
Because that would bring tears of sadness to our eyes.
We will see you again our dearest friends,
Because our friendship will never end.

Yes, it's true we'll be apart for a short while,
But we have something good that holds us together…
Something that has made us better…
Our friendship FOREVER!

We have had our fun, sun, and hotdog buns,
But when we are down with a frown,
We can count on you to be close around.
Why? Because you care and would never let us down.

When the time comes for us to truly go,
We want you to really know
That even though our lives have come to an end,
We will never stop being your friends.
To the end of time…Our love for you extends.

Believe In Yourself
By Thomas Joe Franks

In today's society, it's tough to stand up
For what we believe in at times,
Especially when the odds may be against us!
That is when we must believe in ourselves.
The pressure is on. Resistance is there.
Courage must prevail...I believe in you.

Sometimes, I keep smiling
Even though on the inside I am dying...
While attempting to support others
With all of my available strength.
I believe in you.
You are made of the right stuff.

Some will stop at nothing to put us down,
Even though they know in their hearts
That we are right...We must believe in our ideas.
When we feel with our hearts for others,
We are no longer ordinary, but extraordinary...
My determination is to serve others
With respect and fairness.

Sometimes, I fail in this objective and high aspiration.
I will keep trying until one day I get it right.
I am a vessel under construction. I wish that I was perfect,
But you know and I know and the angels know
That this is NOT true.
My prayer and compassion for you is this:
That (hopefully) I have made your life
A little easier and richer.

Helping people is one of the highest callings.
This takes time and effort,
But is so satisfying, gratifying, and fulfilling.
Your ability, loyalty, and selflessness are superb...
You have given your very best,
Without expecting anything in return!

Hopefully, you know by now that
God cares for you incredibly.
Continue to hold your head up high...
Continue to be the best...Continue to know who you are!
Believe in yourself always.
I have great confidence in you. Better tomorrows await you.
Never give up.
There is nothing that you and God cannot handle.

Winners Never Give Up!
By Thomas Joe Franks

Winners and successful people outlast tough times.
They never see themselves losing.
If you think you will fail, you will.
If you think a situation is hopeless, it probably is.
There is an infallible statement
That the Master Teacher once made,
"Nothing shall be impossible unto you."
Who was He talking about?
He was talking about those that had faith
And truly believed in themselves
And a Supreme Being. You see,
Even the Carpenter had great faith in Himself
He created the Universe.
He knew His purpose, His mission, and His eternal destiny.
Difficult times are only temporary.
When things look so dim and dark, never give up.
Light will shine as the clouds move away.
Someone once said that
"Impossible" is not a valid condition. It's a state of mind."
See yourself winning.

Start talking in a positive manner
Concerning your goals, dreams, and aspirations.
Always keep yourself focused and centered
On your goal and dream.
Surround yourself with positive people
Who can give you positive feedback
Without negative criticism. Be bold
And never, never, never give up.
Winners never give up.
Troubles and setbacks are only temporary.

But great success and victory are permanent milestones.
Winners keep on going in good times, bad times,
Sad times, hard times,
And stormy times. Adversity becomes a challenge.
The only thing that can stop a winner is himself or herself.
Winners are not born.
They are made. They come in all kinds of packages...small,
large, short, tall, black, white, Brown, red, and yellow.
Experience, education, intelligence, money, and talent
Are not Prerequisites to winning.
Winning is a deliberate decision.
It comes from the inside out.
As human beings, we are born to win.
Nonetheless, a decision must be made to be a winner.

That decision can come early in life or late in life.
Some people do not make that decision
Until they are in their mid-sixties.
The difference between a loser
And a winner is "a will to win"
And "a determination to win"
Regardless of how long it takes.
Victory and defeat are sometimes only seconds,
Minutes, or days apart.
The turtle continued in the race.
No one really expected him to win
Against the Swift rabbit, but he did. He persevered.
He continued against all odds.
He had a winner's attitude and... a big heart.
He kept on going and won.
Many times victory is only inches or minutes away.
Thomas Alva Edison had 1000 failures
While trying to invent the light bulb.
Finally, he succeeded. Many people of his day said
That he was a mad, foolish, and Eccentric old man.

The news media wrote all kinds of nasty things about him.
Did he give up? No! Never.
Victory always comes to the winner.

Money
By Thomas Joe Franks

Greater is the wealth that is in YOU
Than the poverty that is in the world.
You have more WEALTH within YOU
Than you will ever need or use.
You have God living within YOU. YOU have Jesus Christ
Living within YOU. YOU have the Holy Spirit LIVING on the
Inside of YOU. How much more wealth do YOU need?
Where are you going to get it?
All WEALTH has been given unto you!
To make or have money, you must have faith in God!
Doubt will steal you blind! Doubt will Kill you financially.
Doubt will create bills when there are none.
Doubt will wipe out a whole family financially.
Doubt is a KILLER. In Caleb's day,
Doubt wiped out a whole generation of wealthy people
(Hundreds of thousands) and their bodies fell dead
In the wilderness. They had money, but they allowed the enemy
To steal it from them... and rip them off!

Take your eyes off the problem. Quit speaking the problem.
Do not speak lack. Remember Caleb?
He was a GIANT of a man in faith.
Even though doubt was all around, he did not speak it.
He spoke of "an EXCEEDING good land...
Flowing with milk and honey.
The people are bread for us. Their defense is gone. The
Lord is with us... fear them not.
They are only wimps.
Their money and land are ours for the taking".
What ever happened to Caleb?
Payday came to his house.

God promised General Caleb and his children
The very land that he had trodden upon
When he had spied out the land.
As a big SUCCESS in finances, Caleb was not shy.
To have money in today's world, you cannot be shy.
The spirit of timidity is not of God. YOU must be BOLD.
Caleb reminded Joshua that he had "WHOLLY followed the Lord".
He wanted what belonged to him.

Caleb demanded his MOUNTAIN of finances. It was payday.
Joshua blessed Caleb and gave him the mountain
That had been promised to him. This particular payday
Was also Caleb's birthday (85 years old). WHAT A PRESENT!
General Caleb had certainly earned it. At last he could
Go in and enjoy his success in finances! He got violent
And seized it. No devil or giant was going to rob or steal
it from him.
He had a made up mind to succeed!
Friend, is your mind made up?
Do YOU want to succeed in finances? If the answer is YES,
Then YOU shall. In short, although we have been given everything in this life
To put us over, we still must go in and possess our money.
Christ has equipped us with gifts, spiritual weapons, wisdom,
Warfare plans (Bible), and POWER through the Holy Spirit.
He has commissioned us to go forth and
Use His POWER to be successful in finances.

The money is ours! But we must seize
The opportunities when possible. We must PRESS OUR WAY IN.
Poverty has to bow at the Name of Jesus.
Your bills will be paid. Successors Are the MIGHTY conquerors,
Not the conquered. YOU are the MIGHTY victor, not the victim.
Poverty is not your master. YOU are its master!

You master poverty by rendering it powerless
And paralyzed in the Name of Jesus.
Get ready. Get EXCITED.
You are God's success for this generation.
You are a winner. You are equipped
With God's power, authority, ability, prosperity, and anointing.
God watches over His Word to perform it and make it happen.
No devil, fool, imp, demon, or person can stop
The 32,000 promises of God. You are a WINNER!
God is FOR you. He is on your side. You are the VICTOR!
You cannot go under for going OVER!

Intolerance Can Be a Beautiful Thing
By Thomas Joe Franks

That's right... Intolerance Can be beautiful thing.
Please don't shut me down
Until you have read the following:

Case in point: Mother Teresa was intolerant of poverty,
So she fed the poor. Abraham Lincoln was intolerant
Of slavery and discrimination against people of color,
So he set them free. David (in the Old Testament) was
Intolerant of Goliath the giant, so he killed him. Christ
was Intolerant of hypocrisy and the wickedness of the
Scribes, Sadducees, and Pharisees, so He called them
hypocrites, Whitewashed tombs full of dead men's
bones, snakes and Vipers, and evil men...so they
killed Him.

General Patton was intolerant of the Nazis
And their ideology, so he and his army
Killed thousands of Germans.
God was intolerant of Sodom and Gomorrah,
So He killed all of them with fire and Brimstone.
Today, we must be intolerant of terrorists,
murderers, rapists, child molesters, cop killers, etc.
The problem is: Most people want to be politically
correct,
Especially when it comes to Abortion,
Partial birth abortions, euthanasia, adultery,
Lying, and cheating.

So what does the average American do? Nothing!
It's time that we become intolerant of evil deeds
And the people who commit them.

You Are God's Lily
By Thomas Joe Franks

You are God's Lily. YOU are not alone. God is with you.
You are one of God's beautiful Lilies
Growing in His flower garden.
God loves Lilies because they are productive and beautiful.
They come back year after year
Even after a long cold winter of adverse weather.
They rise above the ground
And blow freely in the gentle breeze
With the warm sunshine upon their heads.
Lilies are the first to bloom in early spring.
Lilies are flowers of character.
In short, they are strong.
They have an abundance of STRENGTH.
They do not wilt or fall down when the tempest comes.
They brave the storm and ride it out
Like an eagle rides out a hurricane.
Do not fear failure. Failures will happen.
Failure is one of the keys to SUCCESS.
Normally, it is impossible to succeed without failing.
As a child, you fell many times while learning to walk.
It's part of life.
Many times, GREAT SUCCESS is preceded by GREAT
FAILURE.
We must be willing to fail or fall on our face.
Every great man/woman on planet earth has failed.
The important thing is to learn from our failures.
Great success is normally just one tiny step
Beyond our greatest failure.

Heaping Burning Coals on a Person's Head
By Thomas Joe Franks

Heaping burning coals on a person's head...
What does it mean?
"If your enemy is hungry, give him food to eat;
If he is thirsty, give him water to drink.
In doing this, you will heap burning coals on his head,
And the LORD WILL REWARD YOU.
Have you ever had a bad neighbor or
Someone who didn't like you...
For whatever the reason?
In times past, I have. What did I do?

Well, I tried several different approaches...
Being kind, being tough,
Being nice, being a donkey's tail.
But I found out the best approach is found in the Scriptures.
But what does it mean...
"Heaping burning coals on a person's head"?
Well, in Biblical times, every family had a fire
Going in their home or
At least some hot burning coals
In order to cook their meals.
A man was not very responsible
If he let his fire and coals go out.
They did not have matches or lighters in those days.

If your fire or coals went out,
You had to go to your neighbor or
Someone who had some burning hot coals
In their fireplace.
You humbled yourself and asked for help...

In this case, some burning coals to help you
Get your own fire going again.
Normally, your neighbor showed mercy and grace
Toward you and had compassion for you and your family.
You would then take the container
That you brought with you…
And put some burning coals in it…

You would then place the container on your head and
Walk out with thanksgiving in your heart. The Bible says,
"Do not repay evil for evil."
Be careful to do what is right in the eyes of others.
If it is possible…live at peace with everyone.
"Do not take revenge…"
The next verse says to be nice to the person
Who has treated you badly
Because it is like heaping burning coals of fire
On a person's head.
In other words, showing mercy and kindness
To someone who has been bad…
Will eventually win them over…most of the time.

My Loving Dad (Tony)
By Thomas Joe Franks

In the last few days, I have felt like writing about my
father Tony Joe, so here goes: Even though my father
Tony died In 1978, he was and is a father who loves and
respects Human life. He is honest and he never neglects
you or Ignores you.

To me, he is the greatest father that you or I will
ever see.
No other man like him will ever be. He is one of a kind.

When we were scared at night in our bedrooms, he
would Come by to let us know that everything was
alright.

He would say, "Education is very important...so do the
Very best you can in all your classes in school."

Listen to me son,
"Don't hang out with losers on the streets
Because that is not good."
"One day you will become a man.
I want you to do everything you can to succeed."

Our father was like no other man around...
Another man like him just couldn't be found.

It's true...Our fathers carry half of our genetic makeup.
Our relationship with our father plays a huge part of who
We will become. In many segments of society, people
grow Up without ever knowing their fathers. This is
unfortunate Because fathers should play an important

role in raising Their children as mothers do. A father is the model of a Man for his daughter and she will choose a man who is like
Him. A father is the model for his son as well. Fortunately, today there is a trend for fathers
To be more active in their children's lives.

My father Tony Joe was always involved in our lives. He was always fair in his discipline.For example, one day I messed up terribly.
I was bad to the bone. He called me into his office (living room)… and told me that I had screwed up. He asked, "What should be your punishment?" Of course I looked at him and said,
"Dad, I don't know." He looked at me and said, "Your discipline will be three stripes on your back. However, I am going to take your punishment. I want you to take this belt and lay three stripes on my back.
I am going to take your whipping."

Of course, I broke down and cried like a baby…and told Him that I could not whip him with the belt. He looked At me with his bright blue eyes and said, "Thomas Joe, Have you learned your lesson though all of this?" Through Tears, I could hardly answer a weak "Yes". Do you think I ever forgot this? Never…that was almost 60 years ago.

Remembering My Dad (Tony)
By Thomas Joe Franks

I know my father named Tony Joe
Who is so dear to my heart & soul.
Suddenly one day, my life was torn apart.
My father Tony had taught me everything from the start...
And everything that I needed to know...
But I never really listened
Until he had to go.

He gave me so much love and touched my life daily.
Suddenly, it was all over. He was gone.
He taught me right from wrong...
The day he left for Heaven, I wasn't that strong.
He is now gone...and it's so hard to believe,
But this man is my dad who taught me
To achieve and never deceive.

One day, I will see my father again I know.
So, I'll continue to hold him dear and close to my heart...
Because one day when we meet again,
I know we'll never part.
Even though he is gone from earth
To Heaven with a head start,
I can still feel his eternal love,
It's the kind that fits around your heart like a glove.

All the times we spent together,
Growing a love that would last forever...
Are times that will never be forgotten.
I'm sorry about the timing of your death.
I know you didn't want to leave as quickly as you did,
But God called you home to be with Him.

We can make it with God's help. He is by our side.
I know you had more to teach me.
I know you really cared.
Dad, I want you to know today that I truly love you…
And even though you are gone from the earth,
You are not gone from my fond memories of yesterday.

If My Father Was Here, This Is What He Would Say…
By Thomas Joe Franks

"My dear family,
I'm sending this from above,
Remembering all the times we spent together,
Growing a love that would last forever,
Our love for one another will never leave us…
Because we are meant to live forever.
I'm sorry about the timing,
For I didn't want to leave,
But God called me home,
So I departed, but you will see me again.
There was so much left to do,
God took me while I was feeling so young.
I had a loving family,
And so much to teach my sons.
I'm sure you all can make it,
You have God on your side,
And just to let you know,
I'm enjoying this long heavenly ride.
If any of you ever need me,
Just close your eyes and pretend I'm there,
I'll help you through your life.
Hopefully, you remember how much I cared.
I want all of you to know today,
That I love you very much,
And even though I'm gone from the earth,
I can still feel your love."

You Are a Winner
By Thomas Joe Franks

You are a winner. You were born with an infinite value system.
As you matured, you also developed your own values.
You began to see yourself as valuable with great worth.
You began to see yourself as you were created to be.
You began to see yourself with almost "limitless" potential.
As a person of priceless value, significance, and importance,
You soon realized that you did not have to do anything that
Encroached upon your Conscience and sense of ethics.
You began to choose your own goals,
Lifestyle, occupation, and relationships.
Society no longer dictated your destiny. You and God did.
You became responsible for your own actions.
You became a tremendous winner!

Every day is a new challenge.
Every day is a new opportunity.
Every day is a new juncture of excitement.
Every day is a new adventure.
I can hardly wait until tomorrow!
I believe that if we treat others with dignity and respect,
We will be treated in kind.
Life is good! If we sow good things, good words,
And good seeds into the lives of others,
A great harvest will also come to us.
Will you ever experience failure?
Yes, but only on a temporary basis.
Failure does not have to be permanent.
Will failure stop us? No.
We will get up and "keep on trucking".
We will treat failure as a type of fertilizer for Natural growth.
Failure can benefit us only if we allow ourselves

To learn something from it and perhaps… change… if necessary.
You are a winner. You have experienced many victories.
Remind yourself of those victories often.
You are the best "you" that will ever be.

No one can ever produce a better "you" than you… no one!
You have identified the talent that lies within "you"
And your treasured, diamond Potential.
You are now using it as fully as possible toward a purpose
and plan.
This makes you feel good about yourself and worthwhile
Because… at the same time,
You are also benefiting others.
This, my friend, is truly "winning".

Give Love
By Thomas Joe Franks

Give love the right-of-way and see what happens.
It is hard to love hypocrites.
I know Jesus did it, but we are not "Jesus"…
But with His help, we can do it.
What Jesus did, we can do because as Christians,
We have His nature and ability.

If you speak loving words,
But the tone in your voice is sharp and ragged,
You will only exacerbate the issue.
You will need LOVE more as you grow older.
Store it up, accumulate it, and saturate yourself with love.
When the time comes, you will be ready.

One day you will need it and you will have it.
Real love will destroy all that is phony or unreal.
Pretense or façade cannot abide
Where there is genuine love.
Selfishness is destroyed by love…Give Love.
Conquer your world through LOVE.

Jimmy the Blue Crab (Part 1)
By Thomas Joe Franks

You have all heard "fish" stories, but I want to tell you a "crab" story. That's right...a story about a blue crab who we will name "Jimmy". Blue crabs are harvested by using a trap known as a "crab pot". The crab pot is usually made out of wire mesh. The trap contains an entrance for the crabs and normally prohibits exit, but not always. Research has indicated that blue crabs stay together...come hell or high water.

One day, Jimmy was caught in one of these traps with several other blue crabs. Eventually, Jimmy looked around for a way of escape. He looked up and saw that there was no wire mesh at the top of the trap. He decided to go for it; however, the other nineteen crabs decided that Jimmy was staying with them because they had already decided that there was no escape. He ignored their advice and started up the side of the trap. The other crabs caught him and brought him back down to the bottom of the crab pot and told him not to try that again or else. They re-emphasized that there was no way out.

Jimmy waited several hours and then quietly took off up the other side of the trap toward the open top. The other crabs took off after him...caught him...fought with him and cut off one of his crab claws. They told him there was no way of escape from the trap...and if he attempted to escape again, they would take off the other claw.

Jimmy licked his wounds and laid low for a while. He did not want to end up as a crab cake for someone's dinner.

He waited until most of the other crabs were in the far corner of the wire mess trap. Then, he made his move. Even though he only had one claw, Jimmy took off like a bullet toward the wide-open top. He almost made it, but they caught him just as he was about to be free. They fought with him repeatedly…and eventually cut off his other claw.

They said, "Jimmy, we have you now. You will have to stay with us now because you have no claws. We are sorry that you wouldn't listen, but as we told you, there is no way to get out of this trap."

Jimmy replied, "There is no wire mesh on top of this crab pot. It's all open. We can all escape. If we don't, we will be crab cakes by tomorrow evening."

Jimmy waited until he thought they were all asleep. It was very dark, but he knew that he had to make his move now. He began to move very slowly up the side of the trap. He would go a few inches and then stop and look around to insure that no one was after him. He continued to move and then stop and then move some more…getting closer and closer to the top where freedom was awaiting. He finally made it within an inch from freedom when all of a sudden…the biggest and meanest crab…one of the nineteen…grabbed him with both claws and dragged him all the way down to the bottom of the trap again.

They told him there was no way of escape from the trap… and if he attempted to escape again, they would take off the other claw.

Jimmy the Blue Crab (Part 2)

He did not want to end up as a crab cake for someone's dinner. He waited until most of the other crabs were in the far corner of the wire mess trap. Then, he made his move. Even though he only had one claw, Jimmy took off like a bullet toward the wide-open top. He almost made it, but they caught him just as he was about to be free. They fought with him repeatedly...and eventually cut off his other claw.

They said, "Jimmy, we have you now. You will have to stay with us now because you have no claws. We are sorry that you wouldn't listen, but as we told you, there is no way to get out of this trap."

Jimmy replied, "There is no wire mesh on top of this crab pot. It's all open. We can all escape. If we don't, we will be crab cakes by tomorrow evening."

One of the larger crabs spoke up and said, "Jimmy, we know what's best for everyone. No crab has ever escaped from one of these traps. We must all stick together. Now, get some sleep."

Jimmy waited until he thought they were all asleep. It was very dark, but he knew that he had to make his move now. He began to move very slowly up the side of the trap. He would go a few inches and then stop and look around to insure that no one was after him. He continued to move and then stop and then move some more...getting closer and closer to the top where freedom was awaiting. He finally made it within an inch from freedom when all of a sudden...the biggest and meanest crab...one of the nineteen...grabbed him with both claws and dragged him all the way down to the bottom of the trap again.

The crabs all responded, "We told you, but you wouldn't listen. Where did you come up with such a crazy idea that you could escape from this trap? What gave you the idea that there is no wire mesh at the top? Don't you think that we would have known it...if that was the case? Why did you not obey us and stay put? Blue Crabs always stick together...no matter what."

Later, they killed Jimmy because they said he was too radical, extreme, and rebellious. Who ever heard of a crab trap having no top? Of course, Jimmy was right. The trap had no top. He died for his faith, belief, and conviction. What happened to the other nineteen Blue Crabs? They were eaten at a crab feast in Maryland. So what is the moral of the story? Sometimes...actually most of the time, the crowd is wrong. People said that automobiles (horseless carriages) would never replace the horse. People thought that Orville and Wilbur Wright were nuts trying to fly a machine with wings. Others said that Thomas Alva Edison was a Looney Tune trying to make a light bulb. Didn't he know that no one had ever done that before?

So what about you today? Are you up to the challenge of going against the status quo...the run of the mill mediocrity...following the crowd?

YOU ARE NEVER ALONE
By Thomas Joe Franks

You are God's child.
His angels protect you.
May trouble never overtake you.
May you always have plenty of everything.
May your glass always be full.
In your heart know this,
You are never alone.
Heaven has accepted you, but it's not time to go home.

May your tears never come from sorrow,
But always come from laughter.
You are a true friend to so many.
Each passing year, you are refined like pure gold.
Your life is an example of a winner.
You have stayed humble and honorable.
When you smile, you light up the whole room...
Sometimes, the whole city...You are never alone.

You are never alone.
His Spirit is in every beat of your heart.
Sometimes, you will face the unknown,
But not for long.
Wherever you go or whatever you do,
His love for you will follow you always.
Baby you are never alone.
God's love for you will never cease!

Difficult times may come and go.
The strong winds may certainly blow.
So if fear surrounds you, wrap His love around you
Because you are never alone.

Hold your head up high.
Look to the sky.
One day you will fly.
Until then...you are never alone!

To Be A Leader
By Thomas Joe Franks

Remember: To be a leader, thinking positive and thinking radical at times is part of the responsibility and challenge of being on the cutting edge. Basically, we as human beings DO NOT like change. We like things the way they are now...even if they can be improved upon or more efficient. We are safe in NOT rocking the boat. Peter was safe and secure while in the boat with the other eleven. He did not have to walk on the Word of Jesus and the physical water of the Sea of Galilee. But he did. That story has been written into the chronicles of history forever!

Peter was a leader. Galileo was a leader. Martin Luther King was a tremendous leader. Winston Churchill was a great leader. I believe you, too, can become another GREAT leader in our time. You have a Dream, Divine Destiny and Purpose! You are a person of greatness, compassion, love, and prominence. NEVER GIVE UP! You can make it happen…and happen well. So what about you today? Are you up to the challenge of going against the status quo...the run of the mill mediocrity... following the crowd?

The Militant Sentinel
By Thomas Joe Franks

The Sentinel sounds the alarm without vacillation.
He blows the trumpet with joy and exhilaration.
The inhabitants of the land do not hesitate,
But they begin to dedicate and consecrate
Themselves to the great harvest of consummation.
The Day of the Lord comes without equivocation.

The Sentinel shouts, "Charge the enemy without fluctuation.
Our orders are given with authority and illumination."
Each soldier assembles without debate,
And goes forth to protect and defend
The works of domination, intimidation, and manipulation.
General Potentate (Christ) comes to validate the celebration.

America
By Thomas Joe Franks

Let us make America an incredible nation again.
Let us have the opportunity to dream again.
Let us have the freedom and opportunity to work again.
We will continue to honor those who were pioneers
Who lived in danger, but made the path available to us.
Now, our country...our home (America) allows us to be free.

Let us all be dreamers.
America is such a dream come true.
I am so proud to be an American.
Let us have leaders who are STRONG
And filled with love for this great country.
May any tyrants or despots be put to shame.

America is truly a land of liberty and opportunity.
America is blessed by God and His Son...
And the celestial sun, moon, and stars.
His smile is upon our land.
America is truly a land of equality...
red, yellow, brown, black, and white.
Currently, we are a free country...
land of the free and brave.
Let us all pray that our rich Country
Continues to be a land of freedom, opportunity and utopia.

Regardless of the color of your skin, you are an American.
Whether you are poor, rich, middle class, high class
Or in between,
You are a person of hope, dignity, and destiny...
You have a life... a future... a legacy.

America (our beloved country) is still young and growing
By leaps and bounds.
America is still full of hope, strength, and Godly people.
The people who know their God are strong and do exploits.

Heavenly Father, bless America to be an incredible nation again.

It's Beginning To Rain Again
By Thomas Joe Franks

It's beginning to rain again,
My desert soul is being refreshed again.
No more stains of sin remain,
Because the love of Jesus did constrain.
Now the washing of His Blood has proclaimed
The mighty Power in Jesus' Name.

It's beginning to rain again,
The precious Church is being renewed again.
The Holy Spirit has ordained
The early and the latter rain.
Good bye O famine that once restrained;
You've been replaced by the harvest of gain.

It's beginning to rain again,
Planet Earth is being restored again.
Hurts and pains no longer have domain
Because there's Power in Jesus' Name.
God's garden is blooming again;
This final harvest of fruit will remain.

It's beginning to rain again,
My soul is blessed again.
Sweet Anointing, I feel You within.
You've touched my heart again.
Through the power of Jesus' Name,
It's beginning to rain again.

The New Blood Covenant
By Thomas Joe Franks

Adam and Eve received a Covenant of love
Because our Covenant Father is the God above…
Who acted in mercy without hate thereof.
Down through the sands of time,
God looked for another man that would shine
As brightly as the stars and that by design.

Abram was just such a man
In which the Covenant Father could expand
And at the same time this man would understand.
The Blood was shed and blessings proclaimed,
And at last Abram and Sarai had new names acclaimed
That would bring them descendants, fortune, and fame.

As time went on, soon it was apparent and decreed
That a New Blood Covenant would be needed to succeed;
Therefore, the Blood of Jesus did indeed intercede.
Today, our faithful prayers do prevail
Against the enemy who will forever be curtailed.
All hail to King Jesus Whose Blood cannot fail!

The New Blood Covenant gives us class and clout
And makes us a glory spout
Where the power comes out.
The New Blood Covenant makes us free indeed
And today, we are a special combat breed
That goes forth always to decree, lead, and succeed!

I would like to dedicate this poem to all American Military
Service Members everywhere...past and present.

American Service Members
By Thomas Joe Franks

We are American Service Members...the warfighters.
We preserve peace on earth and good will toward men.
We are combat trained and ready to fight again and again!
Do we love our country and the Red, White, and Blue?
Are we proud to serve when called upon to subdue?
As American soldiers, sailors, and airmen,
We do not cotton to flag burners!
We are American warfighters who are combat learners.
We know our country needs us
During times of caution and review.
We breathe, we eat, we sleep, we fight, we bleed,
We love our nation.
We are American fighting men & women
Who have a firm foundation.
Sometimes, we are called upon
To fight a war in a faraway land.
Is freedom really worth it for people who do not understand?
We all know the answer is an emphatic "Yes" and "Amen".
As American soldiers, sailors, and airmen,
We have a calling to be peacemakers on earth.
We travel from country to country...
have seen a lot of dearth...
But we have also seen men and women
And children of great worth!
We have watched our fellow warfighters
Breathe their last breath...
Did we stop and regress? No!
Did we turn coat and run? No!

We are American warfighters that leave no job undone.
We believe in honor, dignity, respect...
Even in death if called upon.
We have to believe that our country needs us today.
We are American warfighters who meditate and pray.
We have faith & believe in the Commander-in-Chief of the Universe always!

<u>Please Note</u>: Soldiers have been around from the beginning of time. Abraham was a soldier. Joshua and Caleb were soldiers. David was a soldier. The New Testament describes soldiers again and again. Paul said, "Endure suffering...as a good soldier of Christ Jesus." Jesus was and is a Soldier...the Commander-in-Chief of the Universe
And will one day rule and reign with a rod of iron.

Believe In Your Dreams!
By Thomas Joe Franks

Whether they are born in the conscious or subconscious,
Your DREAMS are extremely important.
A man without a dream is like a desert without an oasis
Or a summer cloud without rain.
Everyone should have a dream.
Rosa Parks had a dream.
Martin Luther King had a dream.
Bill Gates had a dream.
Harriet Tubman had a dream.
Dream and Believe!
Believe in yourself. Believe in your dreams.
We must have long range dreams that carry us through
short term failures.
Life is not always easy.
Life is part pain, part pleasure, part excitement,
And part mundane,

Dreams are sometimes good, sometimes disappointing,
But never boring.
We can live our lives to our maximum potential
As we dream to the fullest.
The person without a dream is truly not alive...
He is like a walking dead man
With an enemy called "average". You are not average.
You are too knowledgeable and
Too professional to be average.
Dreams help us to develop patience in our lives.
When you have a dream, DO NOT procrastinate, vacillate,
Hesitate, equivocate, or oscillate...continue to move forward.
I would rather have a dream, even if it fails,
Than to have a temporary triumph

That will one day fail...and fade AWAY.
When you dream, dream BIG.
The problem with most dreams is:
They are too small. Great pioneers have great dreams.
Remember this:
Little people talk about other people.
Mediocre people talk about things.
But Great people talk about ideas and their dreams.

You Can Do It, Too!
By Thomas Joe Franks

Don't you dare say "can't".
You can do it, too!
Never give up.
You can do it, too!
Remember the good times.
You can do it, too!
Don't worry about the small stuff.
You can do it, too!
Life can be so beautiful. Why? Because you are in it,
Especially now, because excitement is in the air.
Life is too short to be sad, uneventful, and boring.
A lovely rainbow always comes after the rain. The sun follows.
Therefore, when you feel like you are defeated,
Think positive.
You can do it, too!
Be persistent. Be tough. Don't you dare give up.
You can be successful. It's up to you.
Yes, you can do it, too!

Success
By Thomas Joe Franks

What is SUCCESS in everyday action?
Is it having selfpity of dissatisfaction?
Is it feeling sorry for your reaction?
Is it having a LONG face?
Is it crying the blues in disgrace?
NO...NO...NO...NO!

SUCCESS is laughing in the face of desperation.
SUCCESS is laughing in the face of devastation.
SUCCESS is loving even the belligerent dissident.
SUCCESS is loving even the most impenitent.
Even your critics will inquire
And YOU will be admired.

Some church goers and Christians vacillate.
They seem to find all kinds of ways to procrastinate!
Some have their heads in the clouds
Looking for the rapture as their shroud.
But true SUCCESS is appreciating BEAUTY that is NOW,
The mountains, streams, waterfalls or even a brown cow!

SUCCESS is edifying others.
SUCCESS is comforting others.
SUCCESS is Kingdom Living TODAY...
And will never be far away.
You can heal the sick, cast out devils, captives deliver
Because Jesus is the Healer and Forgiver!

SUCCESS is enthusiasm.
SUCCESS is being in God as a violent involver
And also being a SUCCESS problem resolver.

Go, set people free from the bondage of fear.
Go, activate people and put them in gear.
Go, see them laugh, play, work, and persevere.

True SUCCESS is to die to self and give yourself away.
True SUCCESS is having brought someone into the Kingdom to stay.
True SUCCESS is a living CREATION who is no longer a prey.
Because YOU shared...
Because YOU cared...
Beware, my Love, this is TRUE SUCCESS without despair!

YOU Were Made for Success

By Thomas Joe Franks

YOU were made for GREATNESS!
YOU were made to soar like an eagle...not like a turkey.
YOU were made for excellence.
YOU were made to DOMINATE your circumstances...
Not to be dominated.
YOU have dominion
(The right and power to govern and control).
YOU are a VICTOR...not the victim.
YOU are a GIVER...not a taker.
YOU LOVE...and you love to be loved.
YOU are happy...and filled with JOY.
YOU have Fellowship with God...and HIS children.
YOU are made for SUCCESS!

To Love and Be Loved
By Thomas Joe Franks

Let the past go.
If we are holding on to something
That doesn't belong to us
And it is NOT meant for us, we need to let it go!
If we are still nursing past hurts and pains,
We must let them go.
If someone can't treat us right…love us back…
See our dynamic worth,
We need to let them go.
If someone has angered you, let it go.
If you are thinking of "getting even", let it go.
If you are involved in a wrong relationship or addiction,
Let it go!
If you are holding on to a job that no longer meets your
Needs or talents, let it go.
If you keep judging others to make yourself feel better,
Let it go.
If you have a bad attitude, let it go!
If you are stuck in the past, let it go.
If you keep trying to help someone who will NOT receive
Your help, let it go.
If you are feeling distressed and stressed out, let it go.
If you have been handling a situation all by yourself
And your heart tells you to let it go, Let it GO.

Mercy
By Thomas Joe Franks

What do we know about mercy?
Mercy rearranged my life.
Mercy took away my debt and strife.
Mercy rewrote my name.
Mercy took away the blame.
Mercy saved my life from hell.
Mercy made me whole and well.

What do we know about mercy?
Mercy gave me back my dignity.
Mercy enriched my life significantly.
Mercy, mercy, mercy gave me love
That could only be known from above.
Mercy brings peace, love, and precious gifts
That will stand the test without a rift.

What do we know about mercy?
Mercy brings compassion, forgiveness, & kindness.
Mercy brings light instead of blindness.
Mercy eradicates ignorance & brings understanding.
Mercy brings a soft heart that is less demanding.
Mercy gives and brings goodwill.
Mercy is the good life with a thrill.

What do we know about mercy?
Mercy rearranged my life.
Mercy took away my strife.
Mercy wrote my name above.
Mercy and love go together like a glove.
Where would you and I be without mercy and grace?
We would be hopelessly lost in the big rat race!

God's Money Is Here
By Thomas Joe Franks

God's money is here
And His mercy is dear.
We are His children so near,
And His love is simple without fear.
He spoke of money, it is quite clear,
It is His way of giving earthly cheer!

God's money is here
Somewhat like a crystal chandelier.
It brings light that will appear,
Especially on the dark frontier.
God loves money for He is the Great Financier.
He wants you to revere and ENJOY His atmosphere.

Money be...lack flee...Poverty fall...Jesus calls.
Leanness to the bone...I call you gone.
Slaves of debris...I set you free.
Gates that did assail...will no longer prevail.
In Jesus' Name...I do reclaim...All is mine...I now resign
To come and dine...with Jesus my Divine!"

More From My Heart…
By Thomas Joe Franks

Each of us has a hidden place…
Deep within ourselves…
Somewhere to get away…
To think things through…
To be alone…to have our space.

In our hearts, we confront our deepest feelings…
We hope…
We dream…
Sometimes, we have apprehensions…
Nevertheless, we continue to move forward.

Sometimes, by design…
A Special person discovers a way into our hearts…
That special place we thought was ours alone…
And soon, we allow that person to come in…
And to feel, love, and to share with us.

Do we have passionate emotions about this? Yes!
Do we shut the door on them? No! What happens?
That Special person adds a new perspective
To our hidden place…
Soon, peace and harmony settle down
In this special realm…
Where both will stay forever…And we call this LOVE!

I dedicate this poem to a friend of mine...BILLY BOB.

It is called "Fill Our Hearts with Love".
By Thomas Joe Franks

Love is universal. It unites humanity as one big family.
Truly, it doesn't matter where you find yourself in the world.
You will find people who truly love you as you are...
Like my friend Billy Bob.
Language doesn't matter. Culture doesn't matter.
Rich or poor doesn't matter.
Love is something we all desire. It forms a part of us no
Matter what corner of the world We come from. Sometimes
We may not even speak the same language,
But the power of love is present to unite us.
It can unite two people or families or even nations.
Therefore, we give our love and best affection to you...
Our most beloved Billy Bob.
You have filled our hearts with love.
Billy Bob, you have become a Bright Star.
You light up our pathway.
You brighten the way for many ostentatious souls.

You are the sun that brightens the day for so many
Who have lost their way.
You are the only light that many will ever see.
They see your smile and know that you will support them
During their health issues.
You are their reason for having steadfast faith and hope.
Sometimes, you have shed a tear now and then...
Thinking that no one saw.
In so many instances, you have been the medicine
That was needed to calm the sick.
Today, it's your turn to be cared for...

I have ask your guardian angel and ministering angels
To come on the scene and lift you up.
You are a good Christian Soldier...Billy Bob.
A good heart like yours is very rare...extremely rare.
Since you are from New York City, I would never change
A thing about you.
I believe that God is going to keep you around for a long,
Long time. AMEN!

Our Daughters
By Thomas Joe Franks

I see our daughters
Blossoming as roses in a beautiful garden...
In the early spring...
Growing with each petal that is
Touched by a tiny raindrop...
And even thirsty for more.

I see our daughters
Slowly opening up...
Setting themselves free...
From despair and loneliness,
Free from any guilt or shame.
You are all now responsible young ladies.

I see our daughters
Discovering their beauty
Inside themselves...
And the beauty that surrounds them
At the dawning of each new day.
Each day now brings them bright rays of sunshine.

At times, their lives may have a few clouds,
But the clouds will not cloud their vision.
I see our daughters letting go of negative feelings...
Letting go of any unhappiness.
They are finding out who they really are...
Finding freedom and discovering their beauty.

I see our daughters
Learning to truly love themselves as others already do.

I see them as women growing beyond their wildest dreams...
Beyond their expectations...Filled with awe and excitement...
May you continue to live and grow
Beyond your most incredible dreams.

Exclusively His
By Thomas Joe Franks

The words "Exclusively His" keep going through my mind.
This means that we are made especially for Him all the time.
We belong only to Him.
We have singleness of purpose to please Him.
We are a select group of people who belong to the
Family of God.
That makes us Special.
That makes us Eloquent, Honorable, and Unique.
We are Living Stones filled with His very Presence.
Being exclusively His, we have enthusiasm, zest, and
Incredible motivation.

Our attitude has been adjusted to think like our Father.
We no longer stumble around in the dark.
We know where we have been...
Where we are...and where we are going!
We don't just talk and make a big noise...
We are action people.
We are doers. We encourage. We build up people.
We motivate. We believe.
Nothing can stop you today except one thing...
That's right... one thing... and that is YOU.
No devil can stop you. Individuals cannot stop you. Only
YOU can stop you. Why? Because God is FOR you and is
On your side. You are favored by Him.
There is NOTHING that He will not do for you... NOTHING...
NOTHING...NOTHING.

No More Time For You, Devil
By Thomas Joe Franks

Devil, get out of my way, you hell bent fallen angel.
My time is too valuable to mess around with you.
Your fear and scare tactics don't work here anymore. Why?
Because I have been set free from debt by Jesus Christ
And restored forevermore!

No more time for you, devil...
Don't mess around with me,
If you get in my way, I'll step on you like a flea,
The King of kings takes very good care of me!

Devil, get out of my way; you may roar like a lion,
But you are now toothless and powerless
Running out of time.
The greater One (Jesus) lives inside me because
I have been ransomed from debt
By the Man of Galilee!

Devil, get out my way...because if you don't,
I'll run over you like a steamroller in the scorching sun.
You see, Mr. stupid, I have been redeemed by the Holy One...
Who loves me, cares for me, has set me free...
And has given me the victory!

No more time for you, devil...
Don't mess around with me.
If you get in my way, I'll step on you like a flea,
The King of kings takes very good care of me!

General Jesus Speaks to His Troops
By Thomas Joe Franks

"Now I want you to remember My Word...that no soldier has to die for this universe. Some of you have been wanting to do that, but I must tell you, I have already died for this world. I desire that you live for Me and not die. All My soldiers have already died anyhow. You died at the new birth. I also told you that during famine I would redeem you from death...and in war I would redeem you from the power of the sword. You may not realize this, but there is a real war going on right now all over this land. It is a war between GOOD and evil. The outcome is simple...We win!

As your CommanderinChief, I have raised you up as a great Army that is strong and courageous. You are different and are like no other Army that has ever been or ever will be. The power of the Holy Spirit goes before you. Behind you is a flame of fire that brings warmth and protection to all them that will listen to the beat of My drum. Before you lies a land of plenty and prosperity. To the rear, you leave poverty and lack. When you were children, you thought as children...You behaved as children...You understood as children, but now, you have become grown men and women in My Army.

You are Champions and Winners set in battle array. Under My command, you will not fail. You will take My Holy Word which is the Sword of the Spirit and beat the enemy and all his stupid wimps at their own silly games. You will kick them all the way back to hell. Begin now to dance, sing, and clap your hands. Look the enemy dead in the eye and laugh at his mismanaged and botched tactics.

You have the eye of the tiger and you sound just like the Lion of Judah. You are now a Team...no more ass's head or dove's dung for you (2 Kgs.6:25). The days of weasel pie are over. You are the head and not the tail.

In times past, you neglected and hurt your wounded. That is rapidly coming to a halt. Neither will you break ranks or stab each other in the back. And when the enemy tries to cut you down, you will not be wounded because you are already dead. No one can kill a dead man. The whole earth will shake and quake before you. You will bring terror to the terrorists and fear to the perverted foe. They do not stand a chance. We are not just going to stop the enemy (the devil), but eventually, we are going to send the enemy and his cohorts to the lake of fire forever.

Troops, do your duty. You are going to be fine. You have the finest equipment and armor in the universe. No power on earth or hell can stop you. Prepare for war. Wake up the people. Let them know that it is high time to be a warrior. Advance. Conquer. Destroy. Defeat the diabolical fool (devil) and all of his worthless imps. Kick them when they are up. Kick them when they are down. They don't play fair...so grind them to powder.

Are you ready? Follow Me. We will go forth and wage war in righteousness, holiness, and justice. We will smite the nations and rule with My Scepter of Iron. I will be the world wide Dictator known as the King of kings and Lord of lords. Let's do it. It's final. That's it. PERIOD!"

Christmas at Our House
By Thomas Joe Franks

Christmas is a very special time of year!
Candles and mistletoe are everywhere...
To spread a lot of cheer.
Christmas joy comes from family and friends.
Food and conversations come from women and men.
Christmas brings an inner peaceful light.
There is no substitute for Christmas delight.
Without family, it just doesn't feel right.
Our hearts are one
Because of what our Savior has done!

Christmas is a holiday for family and friends.
We hope this day will never end.
Then we remember the Baby at the Inn.
The three wise men visited Him way back then.
We have all heard about the first Christmas Day.
Even the star of Bethlehem was a huge display.
Christmas is a time for merriment and cheer.
Soon Father Time will bring another year.
The shopping is over...the bills are here.
We don't care because our family is near.

We have made a lot of phone calls, wrapped a lot of gifts,
And wrote several cards.
This day of joy will be remembered in high regards.
If everything was now as it was then...when we were kids
In Zolfo Springs,
Christmas Day would bring a lot of memories,
But not too many things.
Sometimes, I wondered what was going on...
Because Christmas came so quickly and was then gone.

We even knew way back then,
That Christmas was truly about Him, Family, and Friends.
This is the season when we shop at stores even more.
We give to each other because Christmas is an open door
That we cannot ignore!

I Am Going To Do It! Period!
By Thomas Joe Franks

I am going to do it. I have a right.
I've got a responsibility. I am going to do it.
No discussion necessary...No summit meetings.
It's final. That's it. Period.
No question about it. I'm a child of the King.
I refuse mediocrity...No question about it.
I'm a winner. That's the way God made me.
No devil is going to change it.
No man or angel is going to change it.
That's it...No discussion necessary.
I'm moving on. I have a free will. I have a right.
I decide God's way. That's it. No question about it.
It's done. The great victory is won.
The good fight of faith has begun. I'm a winner. Period.
God is changing me.
I'm willing. I'm obedient. I'm ready. I'm available.
I'm committed to Christ. He is my Lord. I am His.
He is mine. That's it. I'm going to do it.
I'm going over the top. No more poverty or lack for me.
Finances and wealth belong to the children of God.
Am I not a child of God?
The Word says, "All things are mine."
No discussion necessary. That's it...Period.
If you don't like it, hide behind a tree and watch.
Let the dogs bark...Let the cats meow.
This Gospel train is moving on...and I'm on it.
I BELIEVE. I RECEIVE. I PERCEIVE. I AM RELIEVED.
The enemy has been defeated...No question about it.
I'm going to do it in the Name of Jesus.
Praise God. Amen!

The Power of His Name
By Thomas Joe Franks

I was lost and living a losing game.
I had no one except me to blame.
He came in and gave me a new name.
He took away all my shame
With the power of His Name.
He gave me a purpose and an inspiring aim.
He lit a fire in my heart and I became a living flame.

He told me that I would never be the same.
He told me that people like me was the reason He came.
I fell down at His feet because now I had everything to gain.
I felt so weak in my physical frame.
My search had now ended for worldly fame.
I now proclaim that He came and took away my shame
By the power of His Name.

You Can Do It!
By Thomas Joe Franks

Don't you dare say "I can't". You can do it.
Never give up. You can do it.
Remember the good times you've had. You can do it.
Don't worry about the small stuff. You can do it.
Life can be so beautiful. Why? Because you are in it
Especially now...because excitement is in the air.
Life is too short to be sad, uneventful, and boring.
A lovely rainbow always comes after the rain.
The sun follows.
Therefore, when you feel like you are defeated,
Think positive. You can do it!
Be persistent. Be tough. Don't you dare give up.
You can be successful. It's up to you. Yes, you can do it!

A Letter to My Son Tony (20 Mar 95)
By Thomas Joe Franks

While I was attending Lee University in TN, your mother and I decided to have another child. On 30 Oct 77 at Ft Benning, GA, that dream became a reality in you, my son. God's hand was upon you from the outset, even while still in your mother's womb. You were the child of promise. Years earlier the Lord had promised me a son. His promise had materialized and you were now a living soul on Planet Earth. I'm sure you are still filled with excitement and ecstasy over your appointment and acceptance to the USAF Academy. Your Mom and I are certainly proud of you and your hard work.

Your backbone and fiber will be tested again and again. Sometimes, you'll feel as if you are in a vice being squeezed like a grapefruit, orange, or lemon. These are the times to make delicious, icecold lemonade. Lemonade is always good during warm or hot elements. Another thought: Diamonds are not made in cool comfortable climates. Diamonds are made in highly pressurized and red hot environments. Even after they are made and mined (discovered), they then must be cut and polished by a master diamond cutter. The Master will do His part if we do ours. Sometimes, you will be called upon to make decisions. All true leaders make decisions. Some of your decisions will be popular, others will not. People do not like to change, nor do they like change, even when it's in their best interest. Over a hundred years ago, Governor Sam Houston of Texas tried to persuade the people of Texas to stay in the Union and not secede from the Union. He told them what would happen to their children if they seceded.

War would take thousands of their sons and devastate their land. Chaos would be the outcome. Nevertheless, they seceded. Rather than be a part of this tragedy, Gov Houston resigned as their governor. We are images of God first and Americans second. You will make courageous and brave decisions for America and you will be successful in implementing those decisions.

I want to take this opportunity to commend you for your exceptional leadership qualities as my first born son. Your influence will be felt upon each of your colleagues and instructors. Your exceptional diplomatic and "confidence building" skills will be highly visible within the USAF Academy. Your unselfish determination in assisting others has produced fruitful and eternal results.
Your Mom and I are proud of you. We love you. Dad

A Letter To My Brother
By Thomas Joe Franks

Dear Brother,
You are not a forgotten Franks Child. You are my brother. Your two brothers and five sisters down here on Earth truly love you. I know life and time for you began during World War II. The place was near Savannah, TN. Even though your journey began with humble beginnings, you are now Heaven's Child and God is very rich toward you. I know you're not sad or fretful because Heaven is a wonderful place. We do miss you though, especially since you checked out early...even before you got a name. Of course, I know they take real good care of you around there.

With all the angels, people, and angelic beings around, I'm sure there's all kinds of excitement, enthusiasm, and love everywhere. One thing for sure, you're never really alone or lonely because God, family members, and friends are near.

Is time in Heaven much different than here on earth? Although you only lived on Planet Earth a few hours after birth, I'm certain you have met our lovely mother by now. Her name is Eva Bearden Franks. You probably see her every day. Have you found her to be a wonderful and holy woman and a sweet lady?

I have a feeling that you and Daddy Tony are also getting acquainted. Do you walk across the golden streets together? You will never be separated again!

Do you ever think about us? If so, please don't worry. We will be just fine. In so many ways, I envy you because I know there is absolutely no harm or danger anywhere on Planet Heaven. I'm confident it is so peaceful where you are.

Tell me something, Brother. Do you play, sing, and laugh a lot up there? One day, we will all come through those gates of pearl. And even though, we are not currently together with you, we know everything is going to be all right. We are on the winning team. All of us are predestined for greatness. We were born to live forever!

Do you walk with the King every day? I'm sure He is so sweet, kind, gentle, and full of love. By the way, did heaven ever give you a name? Do you sing in the heavenly choir or play an instrument in the orchestra?

I miss you, my Brother. Say a prayer for me. I love you. Your brother Thomas Joe

Special Words To You
By Thomas Joe Franks

It's impossible for the sun to stop shining.
It's impossible for the moon to stop reflecting.
It's impossible for the oceans to dry up.
It's impossible for the wind to stop blowing.
It's impossible for a little baby not to cry.
It's impossible for the singing birds not to fly.
It's just impossible for the world to stop turning.
And it's simply just impossible for us to live without
God's love, warmth, care, and kindness...
And all the little things that
He does for us because He loves us!

It's impossible for the time to go backwards.
It's just impossible for Him not to think of us continuously.
It's impossible for us to go on without Him.
It's impossible not to get excited when we hear
His tender voice.
It's impossible for us not to love Him.
It's just impossible for us to think of a world without Him.
Why? I wish I could completely explain it,
But that too is just impossible.
All I know is: God loves you and me with all His heart.
It's just impossible for Him
To deny Himself to His children!

God's Lily
By Thomas Joe Franks

YOU are not alone.
YOU are one of God's Lilies growing in His flower garden.
They come back year after year even after
The long cold winter of adverse weather.
They rise above the ground and blow freely
In the gentle breeze
With the warm sunshine upon their heads.
There are several types of lilies:
The water lily... the Easter lily...
The Lily of the Valley... and the lily pad.
I believe God sees us as His Easter Lilies.
They are the first to bloom in early spring.
Lilies are also flowers of character. In short, they are strong.
They have an abundance of STRENGTH.

They do not wilt or fall down when the tempest comes.
They brave the storm and ride it out
Like an eagle rides out a hurricane.
The Easter Lily is especially aromatic with an aroma
That is pleasant to the sense of smell.
In God's living bouquet of life,
He loves to place His white lilies in strategic areas
In His flower garden.
He has placed YOU in an area
where YOU can bloom and bloom.
You are NOT alone. He has been there with you all the time.
As a lily, you have class. You have style.
After all, your Father owns it all and wants to give it to you...
Simply because He loves you.
You will never be alone again. You are His LILY!

In God's Class
By Thomas Joe Franks

You and I are in God's class.
He made us in His image.
You and I are members of the highest social order
And highest class on this earth and in heaven.
We are in God's Class.
You were made in His direct image.
His fingerprints are all over you.
His DNA is inside you.
He created you in His image.
You are in the same CLASS as God.
You are not God, but you are His child.
You were made in His image.
God will live forever...and so will you!
As a child of God, you will live forever in heaven.
You now have "family status" with God.
You are bone of His Bone...
Flesh of His Flesh...body of His Body,
And the Blood of Jesus Christ His Son flows
Through your veins.
When God looks at YOU, He looks on the inside,
Not on the surface.
God sees the real BEAUTY in YOU. He sees a true WINNER.
You are in God's Class.

To Risk It All
By Thomas Joe Franks

Recently, I read the following anonymous concept:
To laugh is to risk appearing like the fool.
To weep is to risk appearing sentimental.
To reach out for another is to risk involvement.
To expose feelings is to risk exposing our true selves.
To place our ideas, our dreams before a crowd
Is to risk their loss.
To love is to risk not being loved in return.
To live is to risk dying.
To hope is to risk failure.
But risks must be taken! WHY?
Because the greatest hazard in life is to risk nothing.
If we risk nothing and do nothing, we dull our spirits.
We may avoid suffering and sorrow,
But we will not learn, feel, change, grow, love, and live.
If we do not change our attitudes,
We remain chained to them.
In order to grow, we must change
And NOT forfeit our freedom.
Only if we risk...are we truly free.

I wrote this Letter to two of my sisters during Desert Storm

I will share some of it with you. (6 April 91)
By Thomas Joe Franks

Dear Sisters,
This is in response to your last letters. In the past two years, I have been to HELL and back. I KNOW what hell on earth is & what it is not. I am so glad there is a God in Heaven Who knows my heart. At one time, I thought about what would happen if I went to Heaven early before my time was over on this planet, but then I thought about it. That would be pure selfishness & irresponsibility. I have a beautiful family. I couldn't do it! God KNOWS what I have been through! I LOVE you & all my family.

NOW that I am part of Desert Storm, I feel good. I love this beautiful country of ours. I think you would be proud of Major Franks. He seems to be a hard charger and is on first name basis with the Mayor. This war has affected me like no other in history. I sometimes cry over what I have seen. Our mission in support of Desert Storm is to notify the next of kin of those who have died in Saudi Arabia or Mideast. Just a few minutes ago, we notified parents of a soldier who was killed yesterday in a helicopter crash. He was only 32...too young to die! I tried to go to Saudi Arabia, but they wouldn't let me. Instead, they sent me here. I can't help it...I am a SOLDIER at heart.

Recently, I looked into a father's eyes & told him the sad news about his daughter. She was dead...killed as a hero in a vehicle accident. Even now, tears come to my eyes when I remember the look in his eyes (the hurt, anguish, agony, hell). I will go to my grave with his hurt in my heart.

I wish I was coldhearted and could forget, but I can't. Sometimes, I just have to cry, especially when I am alone. Why am I so sensitive? What are these people to me? I don't even KNOW them, yet I awake in the night with their faces before me! I try to be STRONG...and brave...but then I cry. Am I crazy? God, help me! Thousands are returning every week. Many will never make it back home. They will die on the way home! Sometimes, I wish I would have stayed in Zolfo Springs...simple life. I hate death!

Just got a call from W.Va. Some man had read my book on finances. He wanted some free advice. I get calls & letters from all over the world. We all have the same basic needs. My kids think that I am a teddy bear & getting soft...and I guess I am. I can't help it...I love people, even sinners. I meet all kinds of people (saints, sinners, hypocrites, deadheads, airheads, and potheads). God still loves them! Just remember, I love and appreciate all of you & your prayers.

We cannot change people. Only the Holy Spirit can do that. I wish we could. I really do. We cannot change church members. We cannot change ministers. We cannot change spouses. That's the job of the Holy Spirit. Our main responsibility is to take care of our families. And even then, sometimes we fail miserably. I am just a soldier...and a country soldier at that. I love this country. I love America. I will always be indebted to the USA. That's why I will return to government service. My heart is in this country. I am an American fighting soldier. If that is wrong, then I am wrong! People have prayed. You have prayed. We will continue to go forth. I may have been knocked down...but not OUT! I don't write often...so cherish this letter for a while. Thanks again for your prayers.
Love, Your Brother Tommy

God Made You Special
By Thomas Joe Franks

God prepared Heaven for YOU
From the foundation of the world.
God knows you, your ways, your thoughts, your words,
And every hair on your head.
You are the best product that the Father God ever produced.
You mean more to Him than the whole world.
There is nothing that He will NOT do for you...
If It's profitable for you and benefits your life.
God made you special!
You are the "only you".
He formed your inward parts
While you were still in your mother's womb.
You are fearfully and wonderfully made.
God fashioned you, designed you, appointed you,
And brought you into this world.
You are marvelously and incredibly made.
You are the ONLY you that will ever be made or created!
You are made of water, fluid, calcium, iron, carbon, lime,
Fiber, and other tissue. You have 263 bones, 970 miles of
Blood vessels,
20,000 hairs in your ears alone.
You have 10 million nerves and nerve endings,
600 million air cells in your lungs.
Your heart beats 4200 times an hour
And pumps 24,000 pounds of blood every 24 Hours.
Even when you were only an embryo, you were in the mind
Of God.
You are the "apple" of His eye.
You are the BEST product that heaven ever produced.

God has even written a book about you
Which contains all the days of your life.
God planned each of your days before you were born.
You are indeed special to Him!

The Lord of the Dance (Part 1)
By Thomas Joe Franks

When the world began,
I danced with joy in the morning.
I danced in the moonlight with the stars.
I even danced in the warm sunshine from afar.
I came down from heaven and danced on Planet Earth.
At Bethlehem, I had My Birth!

DANCE wherever you may be,
I am (in fact) the Lord of the Dance, said He.
I'll lead every one of you if you will follow Me.
This Jew will teach you all to Dance...and be free.
If you will only respond to Me, you will see
That you too...will DANCE and have JOY through all eternity!

I danced for the sly Scribe
And the ugly Pharisee,
But they would NOT dance
And would NOT follow Me.
I danced for the fishermen as well as James and John.
They came with Me...for their DANCE had begun!

I danced on the Sabbath.
I healed the people and cured the lame.
The "holy" people said, "Ain't that a shame!"
They then whipped Me...stripped Me...ripped Me and hung
Me out to dry...very high.
Yeah, they thought they had Me (Ha)!
They stared at Me with their resentful hearts
And left Me on the Cross to die and to depart.
Little did they know that I would later
Dance with fire and go afar!

I danced on Friday even when the sky turned black.
I danced and I danced. I knew the outcome, Jack.
But let Me tell you something…
It's hard to Dance with the devil on My back.
They buried My Body…and they thought they had Me.
But then I went to hell
And Danced on the devil's back (Ha, Ha).

Oh, that was a good dance. I thought I had died and
Gone to heaven. I continued to dance all over hell.
I danced on the heads of the little imps.
I danced on the heads of the powerless devils.
I said, "Glory! This is fun. I have waited for thousands
Of years for this great moment…and now it's done.
I am the Lord of the Dance!"

The Lord of the Dance (Part 2)

By Thomas Joe Franks

They thought I was gone like a dead tree or bush.
But "I AM…I said, I AM. I AM the Lord of the DANCE…"
And I will be forever FREE…
And I'll go on LOVING You, My Child
So that You too, My beautiful Bride, can be FREE to DANCE
Throughout all eternity. It is your destiny to DANCE!

They cut Me down and I leaped up to heaven…
To join My Father in a "welcome Home Dance".
I am the Life that will NOT die. I am the Lord of the Dance!
I love you and will live with you forever…
But there is one request that I must make.
You must let me lead you in our special Dance.
My Child, can I have this dance with you?

Love and Respect
By Thomas Joe Franks

Love is a two way street.
When we finally accept someone
Even with all our preconceived ideas and limitations...
That's when we accept them for who they are.
We validate them,
Authenticate them,
Confirm them,
Endorse them...no matter what.
The pure love of another is based on trust...simple trust.
We must grow and love from within.
We must trust and love enough
To express authentically our true and honest feelings
As well as our needs.
We need to choose someone who will respect us,
And help us...And listen to us.
Our heart needs to open naturally,
Not in an artificial setting.
Then true love turns into deep love.

We do not need to mold ourselves
To suit the tastes of the other.
This is not true love.
However, we need to respect the other at all times.
From the heart of one lover to the other,
We must learn to relate our feelings to each other.
Love resides passionately where truth
Is expressed without the fear of retribution...
We must accept love whenever it is given.
Love is a precious gift.
We must appreciate it as such and fully acknowledge it.
We must and we shall keep our love alive.

We will love completely and truthfully.
We will confess our shortcomings!
We do have flaws...This is true and no lie.
However, our love will supersede these frailties.
The love of God passes through our beings...
And radiates in our lives because we are alive.
We are filled with love, forgiveness, confidence, and yes...
Humanity!

Top of the Mountain
By Thomas Joe Franks

I have been to the top of the mountain.
In my mind and spirit, I have seen the other side.
The other side is incredibly beautiful
In which mortal words can never completely describe.
Know this: There will be no bombs or guns or weapons
Of mass destruction on the other side of the mountain.
War will be a thing of the past...no more wars.

There will be no more sin or sinners on the other side...
Only born again Christians (children of God).
We will have a brand new name
Given to us by Christ Himself.
The food will be out of this world... delicious,
But not fattening... It will be savory and satisfying.
There will be no light bulbs, flashlights,
Or man-made lights of any type.
Christ will be our Light.

Now get this: No more pain of any kind...
No sickness, disease, health issues, or any kind of illness...
Only total Divine wellness.
No make-up of any kind will be needed.
We will be perfect specimens without any flaws.
Heavenly chariots will be there,
But you won't need them unless
You just want to go for a joy ride.

Travel, time, and space will no longer be an issue.
Time will be no more. WHAT ABOUT MONEY?
You won't need money.
Everything you need will be provided for you at no cost.

If God doesn't have what you want, He will create it for you.
God's children will have everything they desire...There is
NO LACK in Heaven.
Someone asked me about animals.
Animals will also be there.
I personally believe that our dogs and cats
Will be in Heaven.

You Are My Heroes
By Thomas Joe Franks

The people who work… the rich… poor…
The black… white… brown… yellow… and red,
Regardless of your social economic background,
You have worked tirelessly and
Never taken your hands from the plow.
I have seen you take a stand so many times,
While others turned around and fled down
The mountain side.
Oftentimes, you faced the fire alone,
But somehow, you always came forth like a golden throne.
Today, I just want to say,
"You are my Heroes every day!"

I have seen you work ever so hard…
Only to see someone else get the credit
For your report card.
You have honestly given the best years of your life
For your family and this great country of ours…
Without hesitation or strife!
You are my Heroes.
I have watched you grow and weather the storms.
Sometimes, you were in great pain,
But you refused to be crushed or put in chains!

At times, you were perplexed and even harassed,
But you never despaired because you had Class.
You were never afraid to stand up for your fellow coworker.
Even when that person needed a good kick
In the seat of the pants.
You encouraged everyone to stand firm and to be free.
You gave people new hope in their identity and destiny.

You pierced the darkness so that others could see.
You have become beacons of light in this land of the Free.
You are my Heroes!

You have made a better person out of me.
You have given me more faith and passion for life.
You have given me grace and helped me to be
More peaceful during times of strife.
"What makes a Hero?" You asked.
It is doing the right thing when no one is watching.
It is being strong for another when he is weak.
It is giving someone else hope...
When there seems to be no hope.
Look in the mirror...and you will see as I do...
That you are my Heroes indeed!

America Is a Great Land
By Thomas Joe Franks

God is great. America is great.
As we have the opportunity to dream again,
Let us have the freedom to live and hope again.
We honor those who were pioneers before us
Who lived in danger, but made the path available to us.
Now, our home (America) allows us to be
Free and secure within.

Let us all be dreamers.
America is such a dream come true.
I am so proud to be an American.
Let us have leaders who are STRONG
And filled with love for this great country of ours.
May any tyrants or despots be put to shame.

America is truly a land of liberty and opportunity.
America is blessed by God and His Son...
And the celestial sun, moon, and stars.
His smile is upon our land.
America is truly a land of equality...
Red, yellow, brown, black, and white.
Currently, we are a free country...
Land of the free and brave.
Let us all pray that our rich country continues to be a land
Of freedom and opportunity.

Regardless of the color of your skin, you are an American.
Whether you are rich, poor, middle class, or in between,
You are a person of hope, dignity, and destiny...
You have a life...a future...a legacy.
America (our beloved country) is still young and growing

By leaps and bounds.
America is still full of hope, strength, and Godly people,
And people who know their God
Who are strong and do exploits.

America Is a Great Land.

We Can Only Live One Day At A Time!
By Thomas Joe Franks

Today is here with a gentle breeze,
You are a tremendous part of this universe...
Not hidden from sight!
Today is here. May we be graced with various choices...
That perhaps, we never realized we had before.
Today is here. It is ours. Our dreams are not out of reach.
Today, our uncertainty will be transformed into courage.
Our curiosity will prevail.
We will explore deep places within our inner souls.
We will loudly speak truth and honesty.
We will not remain silent when injustice is near.
We will influence people and events.
The world will see our most cherished dreams materialize.
Our passions, dreams, and aspirations will come to pass.
Today is here. We have found the light.
We Can Only Live One Day At A Time.
We have many windows of opportunities.
We have an imagination. We have faith in ourselves.
We will create avenues of success in our lives.
We know today within the core of our being...
That the life we want is here for us,
And belongs to us.
No one can keep it from us...
Not today, Tomorrow or Ever!

The Parable of the Three Trees
Author Unknown

Once upon a time, there were three beautiful green trees.

The first tree named Pine Bark told the other two trees (Peter Maple and Thomas Oak) that he wanted to grow up and be a highly polished treasure chest and hold all kinds of expensive jewels.

The second tree Peter Maple said that he wanted to grow up and be part of a huge ship carrying precious cargo to exotic cities.

The third tree Thomas Oak said that he wanted to grow up and reach for the sky...and be the tallest tree in the forest.

Eventually, Pine Bark grew up and was made into a feeding trough for feeding animals. Pine Bark was NOT very happy about this at all...until one day a young couple came into town. She was with Child...and gave birth to a Son that very night. They needed a crib for the Baby's bed. Pine Bark volunteered to be His crib and bed. After all, this Child was Royalty and the coming King.

Peter Maple also grew up, but instead of becoming a huge ship, he was made into a small fishing boat. He was NOT happy at first, but then one day, a strange thing happened. A Man from Galilee was sleeping in his boat. Suddenly, a storm arose across the lake. The harsh wind was blowing. The rain was relentless. His followers thought that they would perish. The Galilean stood and said, "Peace be still." At this point, Peter Maple knew that the King had come.

This brings us to our third tree Thomas Oak. Some Roman soldiers came to the forest and decided to cut him down. Thomas Oak said, "No, I have not achieved my goal yet, I am still growing and I want to grow even taller and reach for the stars." The soldiers were NOT amused. They cut him down with an ax… then cut him into several pieces…and took him to Jerusalem. As Thomas Oak arrived in Jerusalem, he heard shouting and a huge uproar. He also saw a man beaten, battered, and bruised, Then a Roman soldier said, "Make three crosses and command the Galilean to take one of them to Golgotha." That day Thomas Oak knew his purpose and why he was planted. He would hold and support the King of the Universe for the last six hours of His life. The King died, but after three days, He rose again and went to be with His Father in Heaven…and one day He will come again.

Our Grandchildren
By Thomas Joe Franks

Your lives began in a very special place...America.
You were very small when you arrived...
Yet, so unique and beautiful as a flower
In an elegant and lovely garden.
Because of you, the sky is now gloriously blue.
Never will there be another exactly like you.
Our brilliant sunsets are brighter by far...
The joy you bring into our hearts...sparkles like a star.
We see such splendor...deep within you.
You are so delicate, yet so strong.

You are so special. We have wanted you for so long.
We believe in you...in faith, hope, and love.
You are safe and will continue to grow
With help from above!
We believe in the miracle of you.
From our tender hearts, you are in our thoughts so true.
You are now beginning to really grow like the bamboo.
You are bursting with such incredible life
And energy, we know.
It is now your time to fly high in the sky.
We waited for you for such a long, long time.
At last, we are holding you close in our arms so sublime.

You have a lot of love and awesome charm.
You are such a precious gift so lovely and warm.
You were created and born out of love.
You will live daily with a lot of love from us and above.
Our entire lives have changed because of you,
Especially, from the first moment we had a clue.

You have become the center of great importance and Divine Favor.
You have a brand new life before you today and forever.
You are no longer a blank canvas,
But truly an elegant masterpiece so clever.

Our Identify Versus Our Destiny
By Thomas Joe Franks

Our past failures do not determine our identity or destiny.
Feelings do not determine our identity.
Our jobs and positions do not determine our identity.
However, our identity is somehow
Wrapped up in our destiny.
Dark times come and go,
Even pain sometimes overflows.
We do have an escape...
And the Christ Child is never too late.
What do we do during difficult times?
We remember who we are and continue to be kind.
Since we did not make ourselves, we remember
Whose we are....
He is never away too far.
We must stand for justice, illumination, and light
Because the darkness has no might or insight.
Our Creator will repay us for the years
That the locusts have eaten,
Even though at times, we may feel warn out
And weather-beaten.
The One Who made us has determined
Our value and worth
To be neither average, casual, nor a person of dearth.
We can continue to have peace even during the storm,
Because the sun will shine again tomorrow morn.
We are loved beyond compare.
We can take the mountain...if we dare.
Our identity is not based on our performance or man,
But our destiny is based on our lives
Transformed and enhanced.
Our identity is not based on

Our past failures or circumstance,
Nor is it based on our parents per chance.
Our jobs, skills, and talents do not identify
Who we are in this world so intensified.
Who then, determines our identity and destiny today?
Not only do we, but the Man of Galilee
Also persuades day by day.
He is bigger than any problem we face
In these vessels of clay!

My Favorite Aunt
By Thomas Joe Franks

You are my favorite Aunt who always brightens my day.
You inspire me with everything you do or say.
You are also a lot of fun to be around…
Even when your favorite nephew acts like a clown.
If God had a canvas and He painted you,
He would paint a Christian woman, mother, favorite Aunt,
And a friend so true.
Your picture on canvass would be recognized by everyone.
Your eyes, your spirit, and mild temper second to none…
Would certainly give you away.
Over the years, God has given you a heart as fragrant as
A beautiful bouquet.
Thanks for all of your prayers that you prayed over me.
Without your prayers, I could have been
A complete basket case…you see!

You are my favorite aunt in whom I admire.
No grass ever grows under your feet or tires.
As family, we will always have fond memories of you.
By the way, do you still have that incredible
Red and blue tattoo?
You've brightened our lives with your love
And eternal smile.
Even when we were hostile, you loved us all the while.
No wonder we always liked to come to your house
For coffee or tea!
We want you to stay around a lot longer, we all agree.
You are a great example of what a Christian Mother and
Aunt should be.
Watching you over the years has made us strong.
You remind us that we are children of God's Throne.

You have truly been a wonderful counselor and mentor...
Even on the phone.

Today, I want to tell you that our family loves you.
We think about you often because it's true...
You have brightened our days.
You have brought sunshine into our lives in so many ways.
You have made so many people feel special, extraordinary,
And renewed.
The world has become a better place because of you.
Thank you for sharing your life with us...loving us...and
Caring for us.
Thank you for your advice, prayers,
And your wisdom galore.
Today, this special prayer for you I implore:
"May God bless and keep you and may you live long
Upon this earth. May you Continue to touch the lives
Of your children, grandchildren, and great grandchildren,
And others until you reach your final destination...
Heaven! AMEN."

Remember no one can ever take your place.
When God made you, He threw away the mold...and said,
"I have a woman after My Kind...holy, righteous, and
divine."

My Favorite Aunt (Part 2)

You are my favorite aunt and I know
That I am your favorite nephew.
You have been a phenomenal mother, wonderful wife,
And favorite aunt.
And a fine example of a Christian woman and mother.
The secret is out.
Your love and beauty come from God.
You act tough at times…
But underneath it all, you're a marshmallow.
When you walk into a room,
It suddenly lights up like noon day.
When a crisis comes, you are as cool as a cucumber.
You know the Great I AM will make a way for you and yours.
You have been on your knees many times…

Praying for your children and grandchildren.
For example, when we acted up at times,
And were rapidly becoming basket cases…
You prayed for us…and look at us today.
We still act up at times and speak our minds,
But now we have Jesus as our Lord.
You still have a lot of fire in your eyes
And a lot of joy in your step because you're a woman of God.
Another year has come and gone…so fast…too fast.
And guess what?
Your birthday is here again.
Every time I see you, you grow more dear.

Throughout your 90 years,
You have brought a lot of love and cheer.
Your caring ways have blessed so many lives, far and near.
I am so proud to be your wild and favorite nephew, it's clear.

God has made you into one of His flaming stars.
You will bring brightness wherever you are!
Everyone sees your love for God, your family, and country.
Your love is like a wave
That lifts people higher everyday...
Even when the skies are gray.
Your love will never die or fade away.
Because you are one of God's fiery and favorite bouquets.

Eva Bearden (Mama) Franks, My Mother (Part 1)

By Thomas Joe Franks

Although Mama (Eva) Franks was only a short little woman,
She was wrapped in dynamite...
The power and authority of the Messiah.
She believed in diplomacy,
But she also believed in the "woodshed".
If Mama was unhappy, everybody was unhappy.
She loved her family
And defended them "tooth and toenail".
If Mama wanted to say something,
She said it...and you knew what she had said.
You listened or else...Mama never asked,
"Thomas Joe, are you okay with my decision?
Does this upset you, son?"
Are you kidding me? Hello!
NO, NO! Her decision was final.
When she made a decision,
You shaped up...No discussion necessary!
Mama worked hard...every day.
Mama prayed...every day...Mama smiled...every day.
Mama loved...everyday!
She loved deeply, especially her husband and family.
You didn't want to fool with Mama
Or Mama's family.
If you did, you would be at the mercy of Mama's prayers.
If you were fortunate enough to get on Mama's prayer list,
She would pray you out of hell into Heaven!
She was ruthless in dealing with the devil.
She gave him no ground...Mama was truly a "saint",
But most of all, she was a Godly woman.
And I miss her profoundly...

After all these years (over 50), I still miss her...
Once in a while, I still hear her motherly voice
In the recesses of my mind.
Her spirit and life still go on within me every single day.
I am truly blessed to have such a mother
So sweet, yet feisty...So gentle, yet firm.
So intelligent, yet humble.
Such a great teacher, yet she did not have formal credentials.
So rich in values,
Yet worldly goods were not her ambition.
Mama was a giver of gifts...
She gave gifts to each of us...
Writing, poetry, artistic and technical abilities,
Knowledge, initiative, and education,
Love of people...love of life...and love of God!

Eva Bearden (Mama) Franks, My Mother (Part 2)

By Thomas Joe Franks

My Mother was a poet, a writer, and a scholar.
She never had an enemy...
Her life was filled with hundreds of friends.
I remember in 1950, at our home
In Zolfo Springs, Florida, near Highway 17...
How she gave a sandwich and a glass of tea...
To a bum who was hungry on the street.
She looked him directly in the eyes and said,
"Mister, this is all I have...but you are welcome to it."
Mama also loved cats, dogs, and birds.
Today as I look back, I know how fortunate I really am...
Because of Mama,
I have never done drugs...been in jail or prison...
Fortunately, I was never on welfare...
I have never disrespected my country
Or the American Flag.
Or committed suicide...
She taught me values and principles...
Not with mere words,
But by EXAMPLE.
When I went overseas the first time in 1965...in the Military,
She prayed for me every single day...
Sometimes, several times a day...Oh Yeah!
She was proud of me...I could tell by her letters.
She loved me.
I could see it in her eyes.
One of Mama's last sessions with me
Went something like this:
"You know I love you. I'm not feeling well today.
I want you to be happy.

I want you to always do what's right.
Be ready for the Lord's return, my son.
I love you!"
Today, I still hear her little voice.
She is saying to me,
"Meet me on the other side.
You will like it here too. I am waiting for you.
Remember, always do what's right."
Mama, I love you too...
One of your favorite sons...Thomas Joe.

The Godly Mother
By Thomas Joe Franks

In Memory of my mother: Mrs. Eva (Bearden) Franks

Mother, you are SPECIAL.
You gave me warmth when I was cold.
I was afraid, but you were bold.
My strength had gone,
But YOU were strong.
I had a fever on my brow,
You came and spoke and prayed aloud.
A beautiful smile came upon your face
When you saw the Lord's amazing grace.

Mother, you are SPECIAL.
Your children rise up and call you blessed.
Now, after many years you can get some rest.
Your fervent prayers have stood the test
Because YOU were not afraid to invest.
Abortion never entered your mind.
You are a woman after HIS kind.
Mama, you stormed the gates of hell and won.
Your life in Heaven has begun!

Thoughts Of My Little Brother
Thomas Joe Franks

Dear Little Brother,
You are not a forgotten Child.
You are my brother.
Your two brothers and five sisters
Down here on Planet Earth truly love you.
I know life and time for you began during World War II.
The place was near Savannah, Tennessee.
Even though your journey began with humble beginnings,
You are now Heaven's Child and God is very rich toward you.
I know you're not sad or fretful
Because Heaven is a wonderful place.
We do miss you though,
Especially since you checked out early...
Even before you got a name.
Of course, I know they take real good care of you up there.

With all the angels, people, and angelic beings around there,
I'm sure there's all kinds of excitement,
Enthusiasm, and love everywhere.
One thing for sure,
You're never really alone or lonely...
Because God, family members, and friends are near.
Is time in Heaven much different than on earth?
Although you only lived on Planet Earth a few hours after birth,
I'm certain you have met our lovely mother by now.
Her name is Eva.
You probably see her every day.
Have you found her to be a wonderful
And holy woman and a sweet lady?
I have a feeling that you and Daddy Tony
Are also getting acquainted.

Do you walk across the golden streets together?
You will never be separated again.

Do you ever think about us? If so, please don't worry.
We will be just fine.
I envy you because I know
There is absolutely no harm or danger
Anywhere on Planet Heaven.
I'm confident it is very peaceful where you are.
Tell me something, my dear brother.
Do you play, sing, and laugh a lot up there?
One day, we will all come through those gates of pearl.
And even though, we are not currently together with you,
We know everything is going to be all right.
We are on the winning team.
All of us are predestined for greatness.
We were born to live forever!
Do you walk with the King every day?
I'm sure He is kind, gentle, and full of love.
By the way, did heaven ever give you a name?
Do you sing in the heavenly choir
Or play an instrument in the orchestra?
I miss you, my dear brother. Say a prayer for me. I love you.
Your brother, Thomas Joe

Jesus Is Alive!
By Thomas Joe Franks

About 2000 years ago, the KING was assailed.
They nailed HIM to the cross as an ordinary male.
The earth and universe began to look dark and very pale.
For the moment...the gates of hell
Had exhaled and prevailed
Against the ONE WHO had so often travailed.

The trail of blood had told the tale.
"It is finished," cried the MASTER as the women wailed.
Suddenly, from top to bottom the temple veil
Was torn and rocks were shattered throughout the dale.
It looked as if the imps, devils, and satan would prevail
As they took HIM to their impenetrable jail.

Just hours before, the Son of man had been hailed
As the KING of Israel and even drank from the holy grail.
Now, the people had killed HIM because of false tales.
Would this JESUS ever succeed again and curtail
The wiles and trickery of the FOOL of fools who had haled
Our SWEET JESUS into the pits of hell without bail?

The PRISONER of war had been bruised with much pain.
HIS Life on planet earth had been ordained,
And now HIS Presence in satan's restrain
Would bring great gain to God's ultimate reign.
Time had now expired
For lucifer's insane battle attack against God,
His people, and the SLAIN!

The war was on with battle lines proclaimed,
Even though for three days, the PRISONER was detained.

273

All at once, JESUS shook HIMSELF from satan's campaign
And all hell broke loose with little diabolical brains
Running around like potheads looking for cocaine.
Quickly, the war was over and the paradise lost...
REGAINED.

HE's ALIVE! HE's ALIVE! JESUS of Nazareth was sustained
By the Father and would now rule, reign, and obtain
The Kingdom of all kingdoms that would remain!
JESUS is ALIVE! The crucified ONE could NOT be contained.
Adam the first (made of dust) sold us down the drain,
ADAM the SECOND (JESUS) gave us back
Our rightful domain. AMEN!

Grandma...Washing Clothes
By Thomas Joe Franks

Years ago, I remember my grandmother and even my mother
Having certain recipes for washing clothes.
My Grandmother would first build a fire
Either in the front yard or back...
To heat up the old black kettle.
The water she used was mostly rain water that had run down
From the roof of the house...into an old rain barrel of some type.

Grandma would then set up three galvanized tubs
Or large buckets...
One with clear rinse water,
One with powered starch added in,
And another one for the scrub board in warm, soapy water.
These were all placed strategically
Close to the black and sooty hot kettle.
The tubs had to be set so that the smoke
From the wind did not get in her eyes.
She would then take a bar of lye soap
And shave most of the bar
Into the hot boiling water.

Once, she got the water brewing the way she wanted it,
She would sort out
Two to three piles of clothes
(White, colored, and sometimes work britches or rags).
Next, Grandma would take the white clothes with dirty spots,
Rub them on an old scrub board...And then throw them
Into the boiling kettle.
After boiling for a while,
She would get the broom handle and take
The clothes out of the kettle...then rinse and starch them.

Next, after the clothes were washed, they had to be dried.

She would then lay the towels on the grass,
Hang the work clothes or rags on the fence,
And lay the White clothes on some type
Of hand made "clothes line" made of baling wire.
After drying, they smelled fresh and wonderful...
Like springtime in the morning sun.
Grandma wasn't finished yet.
She would pour the rinse water in the flower
Bed and scrub the front porch with the hot,
Soapy water from the kettle.
The tubs were then turned upside down
By the side of the house.

Last, Grandma would go and put on
A fresh, clean, and ironed dress...
Comb her silky brown hair for her husband, Zack
And brew a mean cup of coffee or tea.
As she sat in her "rocking chair" on the front porch
(After the floor had dried),
She would drink her tea and rock...Baby...rock...
Counting her many, many blessings.
Aren't you thankful today for electric washers and dryers?

2ND Letter To Mama

By Thomas Joe Franks

Hello Mama,

I love you, Mama. Man can do a lot of things on this planet. He can invent. He can educate. He can visualize. But when it comes to making a MOM, only God can do that. Time (sometimes) is our enemy. That's why I want to say these things now to you, Mama...even though you are now in heaven. Yes, I know we have no contact with those of you who have gone on to heaven, but somehow, I believe that God allows you to look in on us occasionally. Perhaps!

Mom, so many words are left unsaid...until it's too late. Does anyone really know why? We as children seem to hold them in our little hearts...and let the years go slipping by. While you were here, I probably never mentioned it very much...how thankful I was for you... being my Mom and all. There was so much I wanted to tell you, but life went by so quickly...so very fast...and then you were gone!

I know even before my birth that you prayed for me. I did not know then how much you would be worth. By the very nature of your motherly attributes, all my basic needs were met. You cared for me; you loved me...even before I knew how valuable a "Mom" could be! Is it too late now to thank you for so many precious things?

Where do I begin? At night, you would read me stories, poems, and the Good Book. You tucked me in so many times. And remember the time I was so sick and how you stood vigil at my bedside? When I was scared and afraid, you always made me feel secure, safe, and loved. You really cared! Mom, many times I was a pain in your backside...like the time I threw a long spiked spear attached to a broom handle at a passing truck… or the time I acted ugly and you almost destroyed the bathroom door to discipline me. I looked into your caring brown eyes and saw that I had caused you much pain.

You were right about so many things, but sometimes I wouldn't listen. After all, I was almost grown…16 years old going on 25. I thought I knew better than you... only to find out later that my immaturity was evident. Tell me something, Mom. How is it that when I tried to sneak in a little white lie or half-truth that you knew? Was it something in my eyes or the way I said it? I'm so sorry. I just did not understand at the time that your rules...were for my own protection. At times, I know you worried about me, especially when I was in the Air Force in France, Germany, and England. You probably thought that I would be sent to Viet Nam one day. You prayed. I traveled. The Lord preserved. I love you, Your son... Thomas Joe

3RD Letter To Mama
By Thomas Joe Franks

Dear Mama,

Mom, today, I have four children of my own. I believe you would be
proud of them. No, they are not perfect...but they have
a lot of you in them. You know, you always did enjoy
the special holidays throughout the year. You made
them so special for us. At Christmas, Daddy would get
the Christmas tree. You would get out the decorations.
All of us would attempt to decorate the tree...and
then Christmas Day would finally dawn...with such
excitement. I remember one year, I received a BB gun.
You were a little hesitant at first, but then you decided
that I was responsible enough to use care and caution.

Did I ever mention the time I shot holes in Tommy
Thomas' bicycle tires? I guess not. Forgive me, Mom.

I've always loved you, Mama. When I get to heaven,
we will sit down and talk about your grandkids. Well,
just the other day, I really wanted to get a hold of your
grandson, Tony. It was not enough for him to dilly-dally
with my expensive computer, but when he came home,
he ran his Toyota truck right into the old oak tree in the
front yard. The tree was fine. No comment on his truck...
not a happy scene.

As you know, I inherited part of your temper. I had to
apologize later to Tony. He's only an overgrown teddy
bear with a heart as big as the Grand Canyon. You would
love him as he would you.

With that being said, if I could have one special wish in my whole life that would come true, this would be my wish: "That my children would love me as much as I have always loved you. Thanks Mom!"

I remember…you always wanted us to brush our teeth and wash our faces every single day. You wanted me to always wear clean underwear…just in case I was in an accident or something. You didn't want them to see me in dirty underwear. Thanks for all the times you bandaged me up when I would skin my knee or elbow or arm. You would always encourage me to keep going. And Mom, I want to thank you for all the times that you continued to help, even though you were so very tired and sick…and didn't want anyone to know. Thanks for checking my pockets before you washed my jeans. Crayons, ink pens, candy, and bubba gum never helped our washing machine.

Thanks for all the hugs you gave me…even the times that I didn't hug you back when I was a teenager. Thanks for not telling Daddy about all the times I acted up and was a pain in your backside. Thanks for being there for me and loving me with your special love as only a Mom could do! And Mama, don't forget to pray for me. I need it! I miss you and love you so much…Your son Thomas Joe

Miraculous Mothers
By Thomas Joe Franks

When the word "mother" is mentioned
The awesome truth prevails.
Some call it magic.
I call it the miraculous!
No other human being affords such comfort to children.
No heart will ever fully understand the connecting bond
Between mother and child.
The Miraculous Mother has such intuition
And "a sixth sense" about her children.
She totally understands
And provides hope, faith, and love for her little ones.
Her love abides. Her hope prevails. Her faith continues.
She provides fertile ground for the child
To dream and laugh and play.
Before long...Chitter Chatter, tiny little finger prints,
And laughter fill the home. AWESOME!
Tenderness and keen sensitivity are characteristic of the
Miraculous Mom.
Her love for her children
Is filled with compassion and great strength.
She is the calm in the storm... The wind in the sails...
The fuel for success!
Mothers bring sweet content and an atmosphere of peace.
It's their nature.
They can also give a "distinct unpleasant look"
At the child when the child has "acted up".
Or use their hand on the child's seat...if necessary.
This too...is love!
Children learn so much from their Moms...
How to play, read, develop goals, smile, and laugh (giggle).
The "bulwark of our nation" is not bullets, beans, or bombs.

It is certainly NOT our government or National Defense. The "bulwark (tower of strength) of our nation" is the Miraculous Mothers. Period!

The hand that rocks the cradle still rules the world. Hello!

The Feeling of Love
By Thomas Joe Franks

For My Son Thomas II & His Wife Hannah...On Their Wedding Celebration

Love is the most incredible feeling.
Love is like a play or romantic movie.
Love is what you feel every day for your partner.
Love is like a smile in the warm sunshine.
Love is like a heartfelt romantic song.
Love is a tremendous emotion
Love keeps you going ever so strong.
Love from the heart speaks volumes…
To your soul mate.
So remember when your eyes meet one another
That you are loving not just with your mind,
But also with your whole heart…
Right from the very start…
Love will keep you…so that you never part.

The Dust Eater
By Thomas Joe Franks

Mr. Slue foot, on the bottom of my shoe you will find
A favorite line of mine.
Since you are the lowlevel dust ball that you are
And a total ignoramus by far,
I don't have to say, "Make my day,"
But I would simply like to convey
Three choking words...Eat my dust,

Because dancing on your head, I must.
You are a dumb defeated foe,
And where you are going is not too cold.
You are indeed so uncouth,
And by far the world's worst nincompoop.
You will spend all eternity in the Lake of Fire,
While we are with the Father and those we admire.

You Were Born To Rule

By Thomas Joe Franks

It is your God given right.
It is inherent within you.
YOU were born to govern and control.
YOU are either ruling or being ruled.
YOU are either dominating or being dominated.
Satan the STUPID one has no power over YOU.
YOU have power to rule.
It is not white power... black power...
Woman power... or man power.
IT IS HOLY GHOST POWER.
"Where the WORD of a king is, there is power" (Eccl. 8:4).
YOU ARE FREE.
YOU ARE WEALTHY.
YOU ARE SUCCESS. YOU ARE WHOLE.
God wants to BLESS EVERYTHING YOU PUT YOUR HAND TO DO.
PROSPERITY IS YOURS. MONEY IS YOURS. ALL THINGS ARE YOURS!

Finances On A Daily Basis
By Thomas Joe Franks

Blessed be the LORDGod forever.
I have given and it is given unto me in good measure,
Pressed down, shaken together, and running over.
I have abundance. I HAVE NO LACK.
MY God meets my needs according to
His riches in glory by Christ Jesus.
The Lord is MY Shepherd. I DO NOT WANT.
Whatever I do shall prosper.
The Lord has restored to me what the devourer has stolen.
I shall eat in plenty and be satisfied.
Praise the Holy Name of Jesus.
I shall never be put to shame.

Whatever my Father has belongs to me
Because I am His child…
And whatever belongs to me belongs to HIM because WE ARE ONE.
I am an heir of God and jointheir with Jesus Christ.
I'm a WINNER, NOT a loser.
I am SUCCESS. I talk SUCCESS. I live SUCCESS.
WHY? Because the WORD works for me.
I believe the WORD rather than lucifer
The loser and all of his lies.
The WORD says that whatever I do shall PROSPER.
I receive financial prosperity NOW...
Thank you Jesus. AMEN.

Money Be...Devil Flee
By Thomas Joe Franks

My Word to you as a money maker is to go forth and give.
The door of poverty will come down.
Your money has been set FREE.
Poverty will NOT prevail against YOU.
But YOU WILL PREVAIL AGAINST POVERTY.
The devil is a LIAR. His power is gone.
God's money is your money. God is your Source.
Money be...devil flee. Money be...lack flee.

Poverty fall...Jesus calls.
Leanness to the bone...I call you gone.
Slaves of debris...I set you free.
Gates that did assail...will no longer prevail.
In Jesus' Name...I do reclaim. All is mine...I now resign...
To come and dine...with Jesus my Divine.
You were born to spend money.
You are worth more than the whole wide world.

God paid a lot for you. You are His most expensive gift.
NOTHING IS TOO GOOD FOR YOU, His child.
Making money is one thing...but, oh, the joy of spending it.
Spending money and giving it away is so exciting.
One day, you will have so much of it until
You will have to ask God what to do with all of it.
You will have to seek His face to KNOW how to spend.
That EXCITES me to no end.
Many Christians have already arrived at this point.
God's people are becoming the most wealthy people on
Planet Earth. AMEN!

Believe In Your Dreams

By Thomas Joe Franks

Whether they are born in the conscious or subconscious,
Your DREAMS are extremely important.
A man without a dream is like a desert without an oasis
Or a summer cloud without rain.
Everyone needs a dream.
Rosa Parks had a dream.
Martin Luther King had a dream.
Bill Gates had a dream.
Harriet Tubman had a dream.
Abraham Lincoln had a dream.
Believe in yourself. Believe in your dreams.
We need long range dreams
To carry us through short term failures.
It will not be easy.

Life is part pain, part pleasure, part excitement, part mundane…
Sometimes good, sometimes disappointing, but never boring.
We can live our lives to our maximum potential
As we dream to the fullest.
The person without a dream is not truly alive.
He is like a walking dead man with an enemy called "average".
Not one of you are average.
You are too knowledgeable to be average.
Dreams require patience in our lives…not procrastination.
Some people procrastinate, vacillate, hesitate,
Equivocate, and oscillate.
That's why we must continue to move forward
Toward our dreams.
I would rather have a dream... even if it fails,
Than to have a temporary triumph
That will one day fail and fade into obscurity.

When you dream, dream BIG.
The problem with most dreams is...They are too small.

Play to Win
By Thomas Joe Franks

We can still play to win even when all odds are against us.
Some will tell us that we don't have a chance in a million.
Only believe. Even when things don't go as planned,
We can still WIN. Sure, sometimes
The breaks seem to go the other way,
But life itself is NOT against you or me. Life is for us.
In our hearts and minds, we can be determined
To approach each day and each adventure
As a glorious gift of golden potential.
As we make things happen for others,
Things will happen for us.

It is an unwritten rule…
It is impossible to help another human being
Without helping ourselves…
After all, we all came from Adam and Eve.
Therefore, when we help another person,
We are actually helping another
Member of our human family that is related to us
In some way. We breathe. We talk.
We walk. We laugh. We work. We play. We live.
Life is a tremendous gift to us.
Each day makes us brand new winners. We live and
experience new and exciting things. Excitement is in the
air. Excitement is everywhere! You are alive! I am alive!
We are alive! Ain't life great?

Speaking as an Orator
By Thomas Joe Franks

Aug 1919, my mother Eva was born. She was born with a cleft palate which meant that she had to have surgery rather young to correct the deformity. Unless she had the operation, she would never be able to speak plainly or communicate in such a way that was understood. She had the surgery. She could now speak with distinction and had lecture type oration...a miracle.

Sep 1946, I was born. I did not have a cleft palate deformity; however, I could not speak plainly until I was eight years old. My classmates would get me to count or talk about some issue just to laugh at me or make fun of me for my poor pronunciation of words. I withstood this humiliation for 8 long years. One day, my mother prayed. She knew about the harassment and mockery... and humiliation. Her prayer was simple: "Lord, stop this humiliation and embarrassment for Thomas Joe's sake. Heal him and make him well so that he can speak fluently, boldly, & confidently."

Another miracle took place. I began to talk and speak with distinction...except for my Southern accent...but that's okay. I was born in the South and I will always be a Southerner. Over the years, I have spoken to dignitaries, VIP's, public figures, General Officers, and thousands of others. With distinction, elegance, and style, I have given over a thousand speeches, homilies, sermons, and seminars in several countries and several states. I was also the spokesman, production manager, and host for several hundred radio programs. Hopefully, I have made a difference in our society because of the miracle of speech.

The month & date: May 1981, Thomas II was born. He had the same problem as I had in the past. He could speak, but not in a way that you understood him. I would go and get his sister Joanna or Tony his brother to interpret for me...so that I could communicate with Thomas. This went on for over seven years. He had a speech therapist that helped, but I knew that it would take another miracle. Many times for many years, I would go into his bedroom when he was already asleep and pray this prayer over him: "Father God, we need your help. I declare and pronounce before You that Thomas II is going to be a great orator, speaker, spokesman, and statesman. I ask You for a miracle... to touch Thomas' tongue and make him well and completely whole. I ask this in Your Name. Amen."

Then one day prior to his 8th birthday, I noticed a miracle. He was speaking boldly and pronouncing his words perfectly...with confidence. Since then, Thomas has spoken with distinction in several countries over several continents that has affected hundreds of lives. You can see him on Facebook making a difference every day. He is a miracle child. Amen.

YOU Were Born to RAZE Hell
By Thomas Joe Franks

YOU were born to RAZE hell (tear down completely, demolish, leave destitute, uncover, erase, and destroy the gates of hell and the works of the devil (1 Jn.3:8).

YOU were born for such a time as this. In the past, the world has laughed at the Church. They have mocked the Church. They have persecuted the Church. But their shenanigans are very rapidly coming to a close.

The most powerful force on this earth, the Church, is NOW shaking herself and becoming the brightest and most valued influence in world affairs. God is resurrecting the Church to be His mighty Army across this land.

God's combat soldiers are beginning to walk in the realm of the miraculous (signs and wonders). You as one of God's soldiers are living in your FINEST hour... invading the impossible and doing things that most people and wimps only dream about.

YOU are destined for GREATNESS. YOU are a WINNER in the war zone. If God be for YOU, who would be so stupid to come against you? YOU are NOW in God's class. How SWEET it is! Live your talk. We must talk right for victory and then walk our talk.

We need to talk healing, health, prosperity, miracles, deliverance, faithfulness, and a whole lot of love. We must speak the oracles of God. You have more POWER locked up in you than you will ever need or use.

The Greater One lives within. He is all powerful and will put you over. Go forth in courage and be fearless as the Lion you serve. He will never fail you. Thank God for Jesus Christ.

Teamwork
By Thomas Joe Franks

Communication is the key that unlocks the door.
Through challenging TEAMWORK, our programs will soar.
Our objectives, mission, and forum, we'll explore.
We must set the tone for many improvements and more.
We must work together as never before.
Professional Team Players are like gold ore.
The hotter the fire and the more you pour,
Each one seems to be refined and shouts, "Encore!"

Teamwork takes pride, action,
And performance as esprit de corps.
Plans and programs are inevitable, we cannot ignore.
Furthermore, with teamwork and professional respect,
We'll make a big score.
Communicating with one another
Provides tremendous results
For the success of Team Camaraderie and more.
You may be a janitor or a doctor or an executor
In a large company store,
But you are still a team player
And a tremendous depositor we cannot ignore.
Yes, you have pride, action, performance,
And esprit de corps.
But with TEAMWORK and mutual respect,
We'll continue to build and restore!
Forevermore!

PS: Remember, Not one of us is as good as all of us.

Printed in the United States
By Bookmasters